Praise for *The Book of*

"This book brings so much validation and clarity to the things my clients and I have been experiencing. I love to read but it seems like so many of the metaphysical books are just the same message with some words changed around. This book both takes you to the next level of evolution and helps you to understand all of the things you are feeling and experiencing at that level. *The Book of Transformation* is fresh and innovative. I would highly recommend it to anyone that is on the spiritual path."

—DJ Ownbey, psychic and coach to the stars

"With *The Book of Transformation*, Lisa Barretta reveals the future of our psychic-spiritual nature that has always seemed illusive and hands us everything we never knew we needed to know. She explains the transformation of our higher consciousness: the ascension into the fifth dimension. This is not a hyped-up account, meant to merely excite us, but an informed commentary of why and how this transformation is taking place (including the origin of humans, the lighting up of our DNA, as well as our connection to the galaxy and alien beings). Barretta includes a stylized encyclopedia of natural ascension tools, such as the use of crystals, stones, oils, chakras, foods, and much more, with specific use for the symptoms we might encounter on our journey. She does this explicitly, matter-of-factly, all the while blending witty comparisons and familiar examples. If ever there was a handbook to ascension, then this is it! I fully endorse this must read for anyone who is living in this exciting time.

—Melissa Leath, author of *Psychic Integrity* and *Outrageous Living*

The Book of Transformation

Open Yourself to Psychic Evolution, the
Rebirth of the World, and the Empowering
Shift Pioneered by the Indigos

Lisa Barretta

New Page Books
A division of The Career Press, Inc.
Pompton Plains, N.J.

THE BOOK OF TRANSFORMATION
EDITED AND TYPESET BY KARA KUMPEL
Cover design by Lucia Rossman/Digi Dog Design
Printed in the U.S.A.

Nothing in this book is intended to take the place of medical advice from a medical professional. But please also consult with a holistic healer who will help you find the energy imbalance in your subtle body that may be aggravating or even causing the physical condition(s).

To order this title, please call toll-free 1-800-CAREER-1 (NJ and Canada: 201-848-0310) to order using VISA or MasterCard, or for further information on books from Career Press.

The Career Press, Inc.
220 West Parkway, Unit 12
Pompton Plains, NJ 07444
www.careerpress.com
www.newpagebooks.com

Library of Congress Cataloging-in-Publication Data
CIP Data Available Upon Request

Evolution is gaining the psychic zones of the world...life, being and ascent of consciousness, could not continue to advance indefinitely along its line without transforming itself in depth. The being who is the object of his own reflection, in consequence, of that very doubling back upon himself becomes in a flash able to raise himself to a new sphere.

—Pierre Teilhard De Chardin

Acknowledgments

Thank you to my parents for the amazing DNA you gave me.

A special acknowledgment to my three muses—my creative, gifted Indigo children: B.J., Alison, and Nick, who were a great source of inspiration for me as I wrote this book.

Bob, the many late-night conversations we had concerning our true celestial heritage were a great inspiration for me as I wrote this book. Your parents, Joe and Anne, are already experiencing life on the other side of the veil where all things are possible. Love transcends time.

And thank you to Michael Pye, my acquisitions editor, who recognized a need for this type of book, and to Kirsten Dalley, for her expertise in editing this work.

Contents

Glossary of Key Terms

Before we get started, take a few minutes to familiarize yourself with the following key terms I use throughout the book.

collective consciousness: A term coined by French sociologist Émile Durkheim (1858–1917) to refer to the shared beliefs and moral attitudes that operate as a unifying force within society. A more current definition in this context is this: "a mode of awareness that emerges at the first transpersonal stage of consciousness, when our identities expand beyond our egos." A crucial capacity that accompanies this awareness is the ability to intuitively sense and work with the interactions between our and others' energy fields—physically, emotionally, mentally, and spiritually. (Source: *www.collectivewisdominitiative.org/papers/kenny_science.htm.*)

Galactic Alignment: The alignment of the December 2012 solstice sun with the Galactic equator. This alignment occurs as a result of the precession of the equinoxes once every 26,000 years, which is what the ancient Maya were pointing to with the 2012 end-date of their Long Count calendar.

Galactic Eye: The center of the Milky Way galaxy, which consists of stars surrounding a black hole.

higher knowing/a higher state of being: An enlightened state that comes from a higher consciousness and having access to dimensions beyond the third dimension.

hit, psychic: A flash of intuitive information. Such hits can include gut feelings, abrupt emotional shifts, dreams, and bodily sensations, just to name a few.

Homo sentient: The next evolutionary stage of *Homo sapiens* that will have bridged the gaps between mind, body, and spirit. This evolved race of humans will have additional "junk" strands of their DNA activated, which in turn will activate psi abilities such as clairvoyance (psychic vision), telepathy, clairaudience (psychic hearing), and clairsentience (psychic sensing). They will also act with compassion and full sentience, bringing about the highest good for all and for the planet.

lightworker: An evolved term for a psychic.

physical thought consciousness: An overly materialistic mindset, with too much emphasis placed on the physical world while discounting the realm of energy and spirit. This is the current state of affairs in the world today.

physio-spiritual form: One's physical and spiritual attributes once they combine into one united frequency.

space-time paradigm: The currently accepted paradigm or worldview in which space, time, and matter constitute the primary (separate) aspects of reality. Within this framework, consciousness is inexplicable. When we evolve, we will realize that consciousness is fundamental and everything else is derivative.

the System: A loosely organized group consisting of governments, religions, and societies that perpetuates the distribution of disinformation regarding our true extraterrestrial origins and advanced abilities.

thoughtforms: Structured interdimensional energies that are the archetypes for our creations.

Preface

The universe is alive with energy that keeps changing, transforming, and creating life. It is a seductive and sensual place indeed. Think about the Big Bang of creation for a moment: Out of a void came this haunting and unfathomable place that eventually conceived the stars, planets, galaxies, and life itself. We are all part of the consciousness factor found in all the matter and energy that makes up this wondrous place. How sexy is that?

Right now we are in the throes of a spiritual revolution that is catapulting us into a new dimension of awareness that transcends the mere material world. In a sense this evolutionary process is very similar to the sexual revolution of the 1960s. Huge changes occurring in our galaxy are pushing us into a kind of spiritual coming-of-age, in which we will be able to see and experience the full creative force of our spirit. The myths and legends about where we came from, who we are, and where we are going are now being discarded to finally reveal the truth about how we are all connected through vibrations and frequencies from the one Divine Source. We are all part of nature and of each other—even our galactic cousins, the so-called alien side of our family tree.

This spiritual awakening, brought about by our planet's position in the galaxy and a radical shift in energy frequency, will encourage us to unshackle ourselves from false beliefs that have held us back for centuries—false beliefs such as *We do not possess extrasensory abilities, we cannot heal ourselves*, and *our world is defined by only three dimensions*. I wrote this book because I want you, dear reader, to understand and appreciate your latent spiritual anatomy, and how the next phase of your evolution will enable you to use your natural psychic abilities and gain a new perspective on the mystical, eternal qualities of consciousness. Knowledge of your true spiritual capabilities will bring self-empowerment, and liberation from the fear-based beliefs and doctrines that have held our spirits captive for far too long by denying our extrasensory, psychic senses in favor of the logical mind.

I will also introduce you to some amazing people who will help you along on your journey, such as the gifted Indigo, Crystal, and Rainbow children, who are attuned to these new frequencies coming into Earth's atmosphere. I will also describe the "tech support" that is available to you through a tightly knit network of spirit guides and even upper-level supervisors, such as the Ascended Masters. And I will tell you about the earthly lightworkers, psychics, holistic practitioners, and metaphysical teachers who are here to help you through the process, as well.

There are tons of books available on how to take care of the physical body and how to recognize and treat the causes and symptoms of physical illness, but this is the very first book that will tell you what to expect—physically, emotionally, mentally, and spiritually—as you evolve into the Aquarian model of your *physio-spiritual form* (that is, your physical and spiritual attributes once they combine into one, united frequency). This book will also help you understand how your physical body is a direct manifestation of what is programmed into your subtle (energy) body. You will realize that deep cellular memory holds the key to your many past life experiences, which, whether you know it or not, are likely still exerting their influence on you.

In some ways this was a difficult book to write, primarily because there is so much I wanted to convey. I was looking at the manual for my cell phone and I saw that it featured a quick-start guide to get the user up and running with the newest features and technology, which can sometimes be confusing to people who aren't "techies," such as me. I was inspired from that little guide to write a book that would more or less be the quick-start guide for the ongoing energy shift and process of transformation into higher consciousness. Because it would be overwhelming for you to have to wade through reams of this once-hidden knowledge all in one dose, I decided it would be better to provide an overview that will hopefully inspire you to delve deeper into your true birthright of vibrational living. I hope that it will motivate you to read other books that may further reveal your true nature, which is one of body and spirit engaged by frequency.

The more fully you open up the portals of higher consciousness, the more you will begin to realize that you are not a victim of the world around you; you are only victimized by the reality that you willingly create and partake in. Your power lies in your consciousness and how you connect to the energy around you. You can create change and manifest a life that is vibrationally attuned to positive living. I wrote this book to assist you in understanding the many dimensional layers of life itself and how to best use your energy to create a world that benefits you, others, and the planet.

This is a fresh look at the spiritual essence in its purest state, which is one of frequency and light. As you begin to shift into self-awareness and explore some of the built-in features of your spirit essence, such as intuition, out-of body experiences, past lives, and chakras, you first must become familiar with how all of these abilities work together to raise your vibration and defeat fear consciousness. The transition into your spiritual awakening requires that you stay grounded while experiencing the Earth's shift into the higher dimensional realms. For peak performance it is essential to upgrade your consciousness by deleting false beliefs and programmed fears as you prepare for your transformation into the multidimensional ascension shift. Hopefully this book will show you how to stay in touch with the universal designer/ manufacturer—the Creator—who gave you all the features necessary for your evolution into the perfection of higher consciousness.

Should you experience any problems during your transformation, I have included sections on maintenance and troubleshooting. For ease of reference I've listed several quick fixes and remedies via crystals, stones, and healing scents for the most common discomforts that are associated with spiritual ascension and awakening. For your own safety, you will also need to know how to recognize and then disconnect from energy vampires who drain your energy, and learn to recognize the signs and symptoms of a psychic attack (or the lesser version, which I call *psi flu*). All too often we get caught up in the cares and requirements of the physical body, and leave the mystery of our energy essence in the category of "if you can't see it, you don't have to deal with it." This is a mistake. The spirit is actually the driving force that informs and animates the human body. That said, the body is still important. When one's spirit energy is down, the body will also start to show outward signs of energetic "misfires" in the form of sickness, physical changes, and even a run of negative experiences. You will also learn that deeply ingrained, intense emotions often have their origins in past lives, and that these emotional imprints often leave clues on your body such as birthmarks and moles.

Finally, you will come to understand how all of your psychic and extrasensory abilities have been hardwired into your physio-spiritual makeup, and how they will facilitate your evolution into a more advanced species. You'll be brought up to speed with the latest features of transformation, including the 22-strand DNA upgrade package and the newly opened psychic eye (the pineal gland)—both of which will help you maneuver more easily in the higher dimensions of expanded consciousness (psychic development and awakening). You will also discover that you have a built-in GPS for your cosmic journey in the form of your enhanced intuitive and telepathic abilities.

This book is an exciting new take on some very old knowledge. It is your physio-spiritual "owner's manual," packed full of interesting information to help you connect the cosmic dots and get a better understanding of spiritual development, maintenance, and ascension as you shift into the new energy field. I am inviting you to feel the power of your spirit essence as it animates and informs your physical body. What would happen if we all knew our own spiritual power? What if we all knew how to embrace the psychic, intuitive side of our nature and use it responsibly? Would we know what to expect from the future if we paid more attention to our psychic impressions and trusted in the validity of such sensations? You are capable of creating the life you've always wanted if you work with both the spiritual and physical aspects of your being. You will learn to live your life intentionally and with enlightenment once you realize how creative you really are.

Are you ready? Grab your cosmic passport as you travel the astral dimensions leading to your ultimate destination of self-discovery, unification, and love.

A Quick-Start Guide for Cosmic Travelers

To fully connect to the universal power source, complete the following quick-start steps before you read the book and embark on your journey:

- ❈ Breathe! Breathing pulls in *prana*, the life force.
- ❈ Keep your feet firmly on the ground or hug a tree to ground any errant or negative energy.
- ❈ Conjure a positive thought and hold it in your mind for at least five minutes.
- ❈ Become aware of how the energy feels in each of your chakra centers. Roll your shoulders to loosen up any psychic kinks.
- ❈ Remember that all problems have solutions, and that your perception is directly controlled by your own thoughts and consciousness.

※ Tap into your intuition to get an answer to your most pressing query—or maybe even a hint of future events!

※ Stretch your arms and lift them above your head. Clasp your hands together and slowly bring them down to your waist. Release your hands and breathe deeply again.

Now you're good to go! Go through these steps periodically as you read to remain fully open to the magic of the universe.

CHAPTER 1

The Sexy Cosmos: Duality and the Dance Toward Enlightenment

There is no doubt that we live in a world of infinite possibilities. As of this writing we are being swept up in a wave of consciousness that will incubate our evolution into the lighter, more psychic, more sentient, more authentic existence we were originally designed for. I say *designed* because it seems unlikely that the DNA molecule developed in only 5 or 6 million years. (Based on the research of the Human Genome Project, it would appear that we had help, in the form of extraterrestrial intervention.) This new wave will advance our evolution as a species and enable us to transcend the limits of the time-space paradigm in which we now operate. This vibrational shift will open a portal to a new, higher awareness that integrates the body, mind, and spirit into one higher, "lighter" frequency, and will give us insight into our

> We live in a world of infinite possibilities.

true genetic lineage along with a panoramic perception of the new world of energy around us.

As I pointed out in the Preface, there is a definite sexiness to the cosmos. We are the creative children of a creative universe. Like toddlers taking their first steps, we are now preparing to leap into the next phase of our evolution, in which we will expand our consciousness and embrace our true spiritual nature. We are shedding our baby fat—the extra weight of that three-dimensional, material-world consciousness—and ascending to become lighter beings who, merely by using the energy of our thoughts and intentions, are capable of manifesting a reality that will benefit everyone. This is not a new concept: Everything that exists was once just an idea that originated in the mind of a dreamer or ideologue, someone who believed in something strongly enough to make it come to fruition so that everyone could share in the use and enjoyment of his or her creations. Pure spiritual alchemy, to say the very least!

> We are the creative children of a creative universe.

The portal to this new energy has been gradually opening up since 1987, the time of the Harmonic Convergence that marked the end of the Hell Cycles of Mayan prophecy.[1] This new, higher frequency will allow us to experience our true mystical and spiritual nature. We will

---

1. Mayan calendar prophecy points to a time of renaissance and planetary quickening linked to the completion of the sun's 26,000-year orbital cycle around the Pleiades star system and the alignment of our winter solstice with the Galactic Center (called the Hunab Ku). These 26,000-year cycles are divided into five sub-periods, called "Suns" by the Maya. As of this writing we are completing the Fourth World/Fifth Sun. Each sub-period/Sun consists of 5,200 years of 360 days each, or 5,125 years of 365.25 days each. Before departing to the east on a raft, the feathered serpent Quetzalcoatl prophesied that there would be 22 cycles, "13 Heavens of Decreasing Choice, followed by Nine Hells of Increasing Doom." Each Heaven and Hell period consists of a 52-year cycle of duration. The 13 Heaven Cycles began in the year AD 843 and ended in 1519, which is when the nine Hell Cycles began. The Hell Cycles ended 468 years later in 1987, the time of the Harmonic Convergence. Quetzalcoatl prophesied that he would return at the end of the 13th Heaven, in 1519. Not coincidentally, this was the exact year that Cortez and the Spaniards arrived in Mexico with their ships bearing a cross,

be the proud possessors of enhanced perception beyond the five physical senses, including instant thought manifestation and superior healing capabilities. All of these once-latent spiritual gifts encoded in our DNA will be ignited by the new waves of energy coming in due to our planet's position within the Milky Way galaxy. As we approach the Galactic Eye (the center of the Milky Way), it will open us up to this elevated consciousness and heightened perception. We are waking up to a brave new world indeed.

> We will be the proud possessors of enhanced perception beyond the five physical senses, including instant thought manifestation and superior healing capabilities.

The entire world seems to be anticipating the Galactic Alignment, the alignment of the December 2012 solstice sun with the Galactic equator, and the mind-blowing experience of expanded consciousness that will result. This alignment is a result of the precession of the equinoxes, something that occurs only once every 26,000 years, and that the ancient Maya were pointing to with the 2012 end-date of their Long Count calendar. These anticipated changes will be global and no longer relegated to the beliefs of a lunatic fringe or false gurus. Enlightenment will be available to all. An elite, secret group hiding behind world governments

---

which was the symbol of Quetzalcoatl's teaching. Aztec Emperor Montezuma II initially believed that the landing of Hernán Cortés in 1519 was Quetzalcoatl's return. The first Hell Cycle commenced with the Spanish brutally conquering and subduing the indigenous population. This also marked the fall of the Aztec Dynasty, as subjugated Indian nations joined with the Spanish to overthrow Aztec rule. The Ninth (and final) Hell Cycle began in 1935, just as Hitler was rising to power in Germany. José Arguelles, known for his role in organizing the Harmonic Convergence and his book The Mayan Factor: Path Beyond Technology, used a mixture of the Aztec and Mayan calendars, and suggested that August 16, 1987, marked the end of the last Hell Cycle, which had begun in AD 1519. The Harmonic Convergence signaled the final 26-year countdown to the end of the Mayan Long Count calendar in 2012, which would mark the end of that cycle and the beginning of a new 5,125-year cycle.

and organized religions has tried its best to suppress this secret knowledge of who we really are, where we came from, and the abilities that we have inherited from the Divine Source. This information will no longer be veiled behind structured beliefs and dogma once we shift into a higher consciousness. We will soon experience the illuminated, spiritual, energetic side of our nature. You are about to find out that you, too, possess the duality of the universe that created you—the complete, innate creative package that is both spiritual and physical.

> We are all still part of one united consciousness.

Philosophers, theologians, and sages throughout the centuries have tried to wrap their heads around the concept that even though we believe ourselves to be separate individuals—islands in the stream—we are all still part of one united consciousness. Admittedly this is a rather weighty concept to digest, but think of it this way: When you hurt someone, you are also hurting yourself. The fact is that we are all connected—globally, galactically, and universally—because we all come from the one creative Source that encompasses both male and female, and is forever creating and expanding. We live inside the universe and the universe lives inside us. We *are* the universe, the microcosm within the macrocosm.

Albert Einstein once said, "Reality is merely an illusion, albeit a very persistent one." The three-dimensional consciousness that exists in the material world is, in essence, an illusion in which the energetic sum total of all our thoughts, feelings, intentions, and expectations is mirrored back to us from a higher plane. Our physicality in the third-dimensional consciousness is a necessary evil, an illusion of separateness, a three-dimensional model of our latent creative and psychic abilities. We are able to see the duality that exists within all of us and experience an existence that we have, quite literally, created just with our thoughts and perceptions. Like the universe itself, we are dualistic in that we can be either positive or negative, and it is our perception—how we choose to view something—that defines its reality to us. Elevated consciousness—that which exists beyond the limitations of three-dimensional consciousness—kicks in when we finally comprehend that we have the choice to create from a more highly evolved thought vibration and therefore design a more harmonious existence for all. Once we truly understand that our intentions sustain our thoughts and bring about results that not only affect us but also the collective consciousness, we will become lighter, more spiritual, more illuminated. We will realize that we need to stop being self-

> We have been trapped in the illusion of materialism.

ish ("it's all about me") and become selfless ("it's all about us") instead. We'll gain a new perspective on ourselves and the world around us; we'll use the positive energy of our thoughts to create a more harmonious outcome. This will be a major step forward in our natural evolutionary progression.

As of this writing, unfortunately, we still live in a world of smoke and mirrors, a world that distorts our perceptions and outright falsifies reality itself. These mirrors are reflecting the inverted image of each and every person back to him- or herself. For this reason we don't always see the true, essential nature of things; we have been trapped in the illusion of materialism. The awakening of your consciousness and the benefits you will reap from it will lay the necessary groundwork to help you start thinking beyond the confines of the physical world. As we become more aware, we will become more psychic and able to understand and interact comfortably with an environment that is, at its most basic level, all about energy and frequency. The lid is coming off the box.

Physical thought consciousness, the kind of thinking that only believes what it can see, is extremely limiting and only leads to confusion, not growth. Conversely, being open to our extrasensory abilities will help us transcend the confines of the material world and enable us to experience the higher dimensions of consciousness beyond the third dimension. Everything we like (and don't like) about ourselves is constantly being shown to us via the manifestation of our thoughts. In other words, whatever we think or feel about ourselves will be mirrored back to us in manifested reality. For example, if you suffer from low self-esteem,

> The opportunity to ascend comes around only once every 26,000 years or so.

this may show up in your life as an unsettling situation or a mean-spirited person. Therefore, you have to ask yourself if you are unconsciously partaking in that unsettling mean-spiritedness: Can you recognize this for what it is—something that you created at one time and that is now being reflected back to you? As you can see, the prime moving force behind all of your creations, whether positive or negative, lies in your intentions, thoughts, and desires.

According to the Maya, the opportunity to ascend comes around only once every 26,000 years or so. In the "in-between" years, only those diligent enough to lead more proactive lifestyles are able to attain this more highly evolved state of being. (Some think that the Maya were able to raise their vibrations to such an extent that they actually transcended their physical bodies and ascended to a higher dimension. But that is a subject for another book.) This particular time of ascension is special: We have not experienced such a major shift in our consciousness since the time of Atlantis, when we were all taking part in a glorious, higher spiritual vibration until arrogance and ego came in and knocked us back down to our "default mode" consciousness of limited third-dimensional reality (some religions describe this as the "fall" of humanity). Because of Earth's position vis-à-vis the Galactic Center, the strands of our DNA that were deactivated at the time of the fall of Atlantis will once again be charged up by the higher frequency.

Of course, our longing to figure out where we came from, who we are, and what our purpose is, is nothing new, so you may be wondering where all of this awakening energy is coming from. It has actually been around for centuries. Once the sole provenance of mystics and sages who knew how to raise their vibrations high enough to detach from the limited, three-dimensional mindset and move beyond the physical world, it is now available to us all. Because of their psychic abilities, these early mystics and sages were thought to have supernatural or magical powers. They seemed to know how to harness the energy of the universe and even bend the laws of nature. They achieved this by studying occult ("hidden") writings, which were made privy to very few at that time. Today, however, globalization and technological advances have allowed for an unprecedented depth and breadth of shared knowledge. We are already experiencing a foretaste of collective consciousness by sharing our knowledge with each other across the globe via the Internet. Structured belief systems, which have traditionally limited our knowledge of this shift in consciousness, will not be able to hold us back for much longer.

> Globalization and technological advances have allowed for an unprecedented depth and breadth of shared knowledge.

The Harmonic Convergence on August 16 and 17, 1987, marked the beginning of a new age, and a significant energy shift in Earth's collective consciousness from warlike to peaceful. Although the stark reality of what is going on in the world today seems to belie this statement, the recent uprisings in the Middle East and the sit-ins against corporate greed show that there is now a unified consciousness working to bring down oppressive governments, corrupt clergy, and falsely structured belief systems, such as those found in banking and finance, that benefit only the select few. The masses are vibrating to the new energy coming in; often, they are being led by the rebellious yet righteous Indigos. After the Harmonic Convergence the new influx of energy began to spur us on toward a unified consciousness; this was when we began to dismantle our old beliefs in earnest and take down the walls that separated us from one another. We are still experiencing this major shift in energy, and when it is complete, it will be a turning point in Earth's collective karma. Once we tune in to this higher frequency, we will evolve as a species and become what we were meant to be: highly aware, multidimensional, psychically gifted members of the human race.

> There is now a unified consciousness working to bring down falsely structured belief systems.

Opening the Portal: Effects of the New Energy

Right now we are all *Homo sapiens* (meaning "wise man" or "knowing man"), so named because we have language and the ability to reason abstractly and solve problems. The human brain mirrors the duality of the universe because it is both logical (left brain) and creative (right brain). The empowering shift will enable us to integrate the left and right sides of our brain to act in unison, which will better equip us to tap into the collective consciousness. The new energy waves that will bring about this empowering shift and finally "conceive" the new man—*Homo sentient*—will commence sometime during 2012. As you read this book, you may find that information you once thought of as esoteric mumbo-jumbo now resonates deeply with you. This means you are ready to make that giant leap forward. It is like going from crawling to walking to running in the space of a day. The energy waves coming through the open portal in the Milky Way will uplift and refine

> The new energy will activate additional strands found in everyone's DNA.

us and put us on the fast track to ascending and evolving as a species. We are shifting out of the Piscean age, the age of religion, due to the precession of the equinoxes, and moving into the Aquarian age, which will be characterized by advanced scientific breakthroughs, spiritual awakening, and the triumph of the ultimate technology, our own psychic senses. *But aren't psychic abilities confined to a select group of gifted people?* you may well ask. The short answer is no. The new energy will activate additional strands found in everyone's DNA. It will be like suddenly and automatically knowing how to use all the apps and commands on your smart phone while getting free, enhanced upgrades. You might say that we will be downloading our multidimensional psychic "apps" and thereby becoming better connected with the entire universe.

Everyone is being affected by the new energy coming in. Even people who don't necessarily seem open to advanced consciousness are, albeit on a very subtle level, now being awakened to the shift in cosmic energy. By way of an example, one day I was standing in line at a local store waiting for my turn to return an item. The person in front of me was giving the cashier a hard time concerning an exchange he wanted to make. At one point I overheard the cashier tell the irate customer that she "didn't like

It is all about energy.

his energy." I smiled to myself and couldn't help but notice that even the little old lady in charge of returns was savvy enough to recognize the importance and omnipresence of energy. It *is* all about energy: our introduction to it, our response to it, and our awareness that it is and always has been our core component. We are all part of the New Response Group (NRG, or "energy"), a term that New Age "insiders" often use to refer to the shift in consciousness brought about by the influx of new energy. The fact that we are privileged enough to be living during this time also means that we will need to learn how to live consciously and mindfully. This is especially true because we will also become more extrasensory and aware of the energy we are sending out and receiving, psychically speaking.

Speaking more personally, you will realize that your creative abilities, the ones you have probably been using unconsciously for years, are now more potent than ever. Your thoughts will also manifest—be made into reality—at a much quicker rate, which will force you to carefully and mindfully consider the quality of those thoughts, or of *thought energy*. Staying grounded and in the moment is of utmost importance during this time. It is all about living consciously and mindfully.

The open energy portal in the Galactic Center will be letting in high-frequency energy waves called *torsion waves*. Torsion waves are energy frequencies that travel at super-radiant speeds throughout the universe, and they may help explain certain psi-related phenomena (for example, telepathy). In the 1950s, Russian astrophysicist Nikolai Kozyrev proved that torsion waves are linked to consciousness,

Your creative abilities are now more potent than ever.

and that our thoughts actually produce these waves. Unfortunately this groundbreaking research was essentially swept under the rug because the idea of unseen

> We are dormant, creative power plants that are on the verge of being woken up.

energy wasn't embraced at that time. It is my belief that these waves combine with the energy of our intentions and thoughts to create reality. We are dormant, creative power plants that are on the verge of being woken up. Once we begin to realize that things don't happen *to* us, but rather *because of* us, we will become much more vigilant regarding our thoughts and intentions.

I work in the psychic profession, so I have been able to get a pretty close look at how people are responding to the new frequency. Many of my clients are open to the existence of psychic abilities. I have had numerous clients tell me about their out-of-body experiences (OBEs), weird synchronicities, lucid dreams, and sharpened instincts when it comes to healing their own bodies. Some have even inadvertently frightened themselves by crossing beyond the veil that separates the material world from the energetic world and communicated with deceased loved ones, interdimensional beings, and spirit guides. What they don't know is that all of these experiences are normal and even necessary if we are to evolve as a species. We need to adapt to this new environment, all the more so because the planet itself will be changing due to its point within the galaxy.

What happens to all of the people who can't or won't resonate with the new vibration? Will they be like birds that become confused and fly into windows? The degree to which each person experiences the energy shift all depends on his or her stage of spiritual evolution, and how open he or she is to the idea and the process of change. The stark reality is that those who choose to remain at a lower vibration, either because of resistance to change or fear of letting go of the old belief systems, may find it difficult to cope with this shift in energy. In order to thrive under these new circumstances we must accept the fact that everything changes as it evolves. For example, not

> We will be the next upgrade in the communications field.

too long ago the idea of the telephone seemed far-fetched; now, however, because of our many advancements in technology, the standard land-line phone seems obsolete and even silly when compared to computers and smart phones. Wait until our telepathic abilities become fully charged as a result of our expanded consciousness—goodbye, cell phone contracts! *We* will be the next upgrade in the communications field. Psi abilities such as *clairvoyance* (clear vision), *telekinesis* (moving objects with one's thoughts), *teleportation* (exiting one physical universe or plane of existence and then re-entering it at a different location), *telepathy* (communicating without the use of speech), *clairaudience* (clear hearing), and *clairsentience* (clear sense) will all be possible as we embrace this shift and become acclimated to the new frequency.

Mind Over Matter?

Some people are under the impression that the shift into a higher consciousness means that the material world will disappear. That's simply untrue. The fact that we are becoming more energetic and spiritual doesn't mean that the material world will cease to exist. One way to understand how this

> The material world will simply become less significant.

works is to think of three-dimensional shapes: Just because these shapes exist doesn't mean that one-dimensional lines and points cease to exist. As we evolve and become more attuned to the "light" energy of our thoughts, as opposed to the "heavy" energy of the material world, the material world will simply become *less significant*. Just because we are becoming more energetic doesn't mean that we will lose our physical bodies; rather, we will have a more complete understanding of how our thoughts are responsible for shaping both our bodies and the world in which we live.

Staying Grounded in the Moment

When we stay in the moment we are actually experiencing the fourth dimension of space-time, or nonlinear time, in which what we project in the form of our thoughts is cast back down to our three-dimensional world as a shadow or illusory reality. The fourth dimension is where we think outside of the limitations of the three-dimensional box of the physical world. We experience the fourth dimension in dreams, during OBEs, and during other vibrational shifts such as déjà vu. This dimension is our "bridge zone" that helps us become acclimated to the higher frequencies that will soon be a familiar part of our advancement. Eventually we will be able to move past the fourth dimension and into the fifth dimension of consciousness—what the Hopi Indians called the Fifth World or Day of Purification. The Maya anticipated that this would occur at the end of a 26,000-year astronomic cycle and would create a new opportunity for the transformation of humanity's consciousness. In the fifth dimension anything and everything is possible. We won't need to engage in the lower-consciousness struggle for control, nor will we need to impose limitations upon ourselves or others; rather, we will simply exist as free, creative spirits who no longer need to attach themselves to heavily weighted material things in order to have an identity. In fact, the ego itself will be obliterated entirely because there will no longer be any need for that false shield to protect the once-vulnerable spirit. We are evolving to be our authentic selves, vibrating to the higher frequencies of light, truth, and love.

The infinite intelligence that resides within each of us is currently being sparked. We are returning to our true nature, which is spirit energy. Our ability to manifest our thoughts into matter via creative visualization is one of the most significant extrasensory capabilities we have. For this reason, it is of the utmost importance that we live mindfully. When we become aware of how our thoughts can shape our personal reality (and, on a larger scale, the collective reality of our planet), we will appreciate the value of staying in the moment. Admittedly, staying in the moment is an incredibly difficult thing to do. The world today moves at such as fast pace that our thoughts often race ahead of us.

> We are evolving to be our authentic selves, vibrating to the higher frequencies of light, truth, and love.

The antidote for this all-too-common malaise is to start being conscious of the thoughts we are projecting. As we evolve, our ability to manifest our thoughts will become more and more finely honed. Every thought that we have is actually "seeding" the future. Therefore, it is imperative that we recognize our newly awakened creative abilities and understand how the law of attraction, thought projection, creative visualization, and torsion waves all work together to manifest the world we live in.

The third dimension of consciousness is where energy slows down enough to take form and become matter. It is easy to get stuck in this phase of consciousness if you have formed attachments to the things that you have created; this, in turn, defines and hence limits you, and causes you to over-identify with the material world. Therefore you need to be cognizant of the intentions of the creative energy behind each and every thought. Every thought that you conceive is "birthed" somewhere down the line as a created reality; if you are not grounded in the moment, your thoughts are likely to become distorted and show up as unintended or unwanted realities. The trick to manifesting your thoughts and bringing about what you desire is intention combined with staying in the moment. The intention behind the thought is what colors the outcome. Once you realize that your multidimensional capabilities are fully accessible to you, you will begin to understand how your perceptions are directly influenced by your thoughts. Is the glass half-empty or half-full? *You* are the deciding factor. The vibration and frequency of your own thoughts will determine the outcome of every situation.

Re-read those last few sentences a few times and let it all sink in.

Jealousy, greed, competitiveness, and other fear-based feelings will not sustain you for very long because the new frequencies coming in are of a higher vibration and thus won't resonate with those lower "fear-factor" vibes. In other words, if you go around thinking negative thoughts and living in victim consciousness, you will embody and live in a world of constant low vibrations (read: negativity). Likewise, if and when you shift gears and amp up your vibration, you will not only look and feel better but you will also begin to have a better relationship with your environment.

Say, for instance, that you find yourself in a tight financial situation (which I am sure most of us can relate to these days). By panicking and focusing on your lack of money or how you can't pay your bills, you are actually bringing about the undesired results of falling short financially. If you are like most people, you are probably unaware that you've been creating your lack of financial security by projecting negative thoughts that are fear-based and limiting. If the intentions behind your thoughts are all fear-based, the strong emotion of fear will manifest more of the same unwanted results. As difficult as it may seem at times, you must stay in the moment, because fear is, by definition, an anxious projection into future events. Only by living in the moment can you control your thoughts and hence the outcome you desire. It can be difficult not to let your emotions take over when you are trying to stay positive in an already-negative situation. You must be disciplined and focused enough to *control what you create*. As with anything else, this takes practice and repetition.

Control what you create.

Because we are energy beings first and foremost, the process of grounding is important—especially now that our psychic energy sensors are becoming more acute. Grounding is one way of staying in the moment and not letting your energy get diverted into a projected future outcome. You may have heard the saying "Don't focus on what you don't want; focus on what you *do* want." Stay in the moment. Remain positive and avoid thinking about or saying anything negative. Phrase your desires positively as affirmations. By saying things like "I will never be debt-free," or, "I don't feel well," you actually wind up creating more of those unwanted negative circumstances. So put aside the negative words and instead choose to start consciously phrasing your desires in a more positive way. For example, when it comes to your finances, say, "I am financially free." With regard to your health, say, "I am in good health." Even in cases of catastrophic illness or injury, relief and even complete healing can be brought about by a change in thinking. (I will get into our ability to self-heal a little later in the book.)

Stay in the moment.

According to author Louise Hay, every disease (*dis-ease*) starts out as a thought vibration. It's critical that you eliminate the negative, because such thoughts and statements tend to materialize rather quickly.

Here are a few things that you can do to stay in the moment and create the outcomes you desire. As you work with all of your newly ignited energetic, spiritual, and creative abilities, watch how quickly and magically you will create the positive results you want:

❋ Avoid negative thoughts, situations, and people.

❋ Retain a sense of calm, even in tough situations. This is actually fairly easy to do if you realize that third-dimension reality is basically an illusion. Focus on solutions, not problems.

❋ Focus on your breathing; feel every breath.

❋ Drop imaginary grounding cords down into the ground.

❋ Bring your awareness to the moment at hand, and don't let your mind wander into the past or future. Experience the fullness of the Now. Take note of your surroundings and allow yourself to really feel the energy around you.

❋ If you begin to project too far into the future or get stuck in the past, tap yourself three times on each shoulder; this will help reset your conscious to the Now.

Who Are the Indigo, Crystal, and Rainbow Children?

Upgrading to the next level of consciousness is part of our evolution as a species. We are becoming more crystal- or light-based than carbon-based.[2] The first manifestations of this lighter *Homo sentient* ("feeling man"—as opposed to *Homo sapiens*, "thinking man") were the Indigo,

---

2. The higher frequencies entering in through the Galactic Center are activating the extra strands of our DNA formerly known as "junk" DNA. The structure of our DNA is actually changing to code to the frequency of light or energy, not just proteins. We will soon be able to experience both the physical world and the higher dimensions of consciousness where the psychic realms give us a broader perspective on our created reality.

Crystal, and Rainbow children that began arriving in the 1980s. Here, I'll explain a little bit about these amazing beings and their impact on our evolution.

Upgrading to the next level of consciousness is part of our evolution as a species.

The Indigo Children

It is natural for each successive generation to differ from the previous one in terms of how they think, act, and even look. When we look back at the lives that our parents and grandparents lived, it becomes apparent just how sweeping this kind of change can be. Ideally we all would like to think that our progeny will make the world a better place in the future. Most parents think that their children are special, but the new wave of children who began arriving in droves in the late 1970s and '80s were indeed special: They were the Indigo children (now Indigo adults, of course).

Lee Carroll and Jan Tober, authors of *The Indigo Children: The New Kids Have Arrived*, were the first to coin the term *Indigo* in 1999. According to Carroll and Tober, the Indigo children were born when Earth was just beginning to pull in those new energy waves from the Milky Way. These children were born into a newly opened gateway of higher-frequency energy coming into Earth's atmosphere. This new frequency activated certain codes lying dormant in their DNA. Carroll and Tober called them Indigos because their auras are composed primarily of this color. This is also the color associated with the Third Eye chakra between the eyes (sometimes called the Brow chakra), which rules the realm of wisdom, intuition, and second sight (also known as *clairvoyance*). This chakra is where we discern truth, develop intuition, and fine-tune our perception. Indigo children are born with this chakra already activated; what are latent or learned psychic abilities in some people are natural gifts for these children.

Although this influx in the '70s and '80s was the biggest of its kind, other Indigos have been born into this world throughout the centuries; it was necessary to have some progressive thinkers lay the groundwork for the generations to come. Like their later counterparts, these early

Indigos were already tuned to a higher vibration, most likely because they were former Atlanteans. They were master beings who agreed to be reincarnated to preserve the teachings of the cosmos by returning to Earth to deliver their messages and knowledge. These reincarnated Indigo souls were the Greek philosophers, the Renaissance painters, the musicians, the writers, the notable inventors and scientists, and people of renown who came to change humanity for the better so we could all advance and ascend to a higher state of consciousness. They were the precursors to what is now a major part of our world's population and basically the next phase of our evolution and ascension as a species.

The new children born in the latter part of the 1970s came ready to speak the truth, to dismantle old, structured, antiquated beliefs, and to pave the way for the expansion of our extrasensory abilities, especially the *psychic eye* (the pineal gland, the hub of our psychic senses). They were and still are often misunderstood, and seen as troubled warriors or oversensitive rebels who are difficult to deal with. The truth is that because Indigos are so psychic, sensitive, and truthful, they are highly intolerant of anything false or phony. For this reason they often seem to overreact to perceived unfairness and have little patience for rules, discipline, authority, or the "old regime." Rather than censure them, we need to realize that they are here to help clear the way for the ascension process to move us out of fear-based consciousness.

Many Indigos have strong memory recall from the time of Atlantis. Indeed, this is what makes them so emotionally and spiritually sensitive: They intuitively remember all that has gone before and know what issues need to be resolved and changed to bring about a better vibration to enable Earth and her inhabitants to shift up to a higher consciousness. Other Indigos who have not had as many life incarnations may appear tough and more warrior-like because they do not have very many emotional energy cords connecting them to this life. They have few or no attachments to the past so they can easily discard what is unnecessary or even harmful. In this

> Indigos are intolerant of anything false or phony.

sense they are much more practical than their earlier counterparts, ready to roll up their sleeves and get to work to tear down the old structured systems, relationships, and conditions that just aren't sustainable in a world of higher vibration. Newly incarnated Indigos are usually the more impatient of the two groups; they are eager to prepare Earth and its inhabitants for a much-needed karmic clean-up. They want to help free us from those reassuring but limiting beliefs that keep us trapped in fear-based consciousness. By way of analogy, you probably know how difficult it is to clean out your closet because of the emotional attachments you have to certain items of clothing. When a friend helps you weed through your stuff, however, you can get up-to-date and organized in no time. The Indigos are like those friends—helpers in the process of clearing out the old and bringing in the new. Many once-established systems, governments, religions, and prejudices have been dismantled because of the influence of Indigos on world history.

So how do you know whether you are an Indigo or possibly the parent or relative of one of these upgraded *Homo sapiens*? Along with being intuitive, creative, independent, and sensitive to processed foods (which I will address in a later chapter), Indigos all seem to share the following characteristics:

- ❋ Difficulty with authority and rules.
- ❋ Impatient and easily bored.
- ❋ Nonconformists; march to the beat of their own drummer.
- ❋ Great multitaskers.
- ❋ Often misdiagnosed as having ADD (attention deficit disorder).
- ❋ Gifted, talented, highly intelligent; often learn to read before school age.
- ❋ Spiritual rather than religious.
- ❋ Easily angered at injustice to others, animals, and the environment.
- ❋ Right-brained and creative, rather than left-brained and logical.
- ❋ Usually have trouble with traditional schooling; learn more easily in advanced or creative classes.

❉   Often a part of misunderstood groups and subcultures (for example, Goth culture).

❉   Technologically inclined.

❉   Blessed with boundless energy.

Unfortunately, Indigos are not always seen in the best light. Oftentimes they have been fed the wrong food (usually processed and/or contaminated with chemicals) and overly medicated (with Ritalin and Prozac, for example) by a system that is either not ready to deal with them or, in a much more sinister scenario, is purposefully attempting to silence their voices. Such poor souls become statistics for depression (anger turned inward), violent crime, and even suicide. Remember that Indigos are spiritual warriors, and their natural urge to fight for a cause can misfire and cause havoc if their energy is tampered with. Drugging this group distorts their psychic energy and can cause frequency blackouts. (A frequency blackout is akin to losing a connection with a power source.) This can cause them to act more from the dark instead of the light. For example, Indigos who have been labeled with behavioral problems as children often grow into adults who have deep emotional wounds, which causes them to become radical social misfits who thrive on disruption.

The Crystal Children

The next advance in our spiritual evolution came with the advent of the Crystal children. Most of these highly sensitive "upgrades" to the human species began to arrive in the mid-1990s, although Crystal vibrations have incarnated at various times throughout the history of our planet. Crystals who arrived on Earth prematurely found that existing in the lower vibrations of three-dimensional earthly consciousnesses was too difficult, so they usually lived very short lives and checked out early, either from suicide or simply by losing their will to live and manifesting a serious illness. They were often considered to be

> Crystal children are extremely placid and calm.

mystical, pure, almost angelic or saintly in nature. Unlike the warrior Indigos, Crystal children are extremely placid and calm. Both physically and emotionally delicate, they are very much in tune with the changing waves of energy that make us more sentient when it comes to experiencing psychic energy. The Crystals don't need to physically fight to show resistance; they simply adjust their thought waves to bring about a desired result. Crystal children are sometimes labeled as autistic or savant because people generally don't understand how they communicate or think. Crystals are certainly less vocal than their predecessors, the Indigos. They communicate telepathically, which is what often results in the misdiagnosis of autism. They are also extremely sensitive to sound frequencies and loud noises; harsh words and erratic vibrations irritate them. Crystal children have crystalline auras or energy fields, which are both reflective of and enhanced by light. The auras of these children have the same properties of clear quartz crystal in that they resonate with and amplify the energy around them. Sensitive Crystal children are peace-loving; disharmony in their immediate environment exhausts them emotionally. People with Crystal auras thrive in calm settings and often become ill if exposed to angry, stressful situations. Like the Indigos, their innate psychic and telepathic abilities enable them to detect lies and see through the false belief structures created by dogmatic religions, controlling governments, and hypocritical people.

Crystal children are born with an advanced Crown chakra. Located at the very top of the head, this chakra is associated with Divine wisdom. They also possess the entirely new Eighth chakra, which connects the spirit essence into the higher dimensions of universal love. Crystal children come here with a clean slate, free from any baggage. The very few who came into Earth's three-dimensional consciousness in previous centuries did not accumulate any karma to be corrected. They came as examples to show us how an evolved being behaves and

> Crystal children possess the entirely new Eighth chakra, which connects the spirit essence into the higher dimensions of universal love.

resonates to the higher frequencies of love and peace. Those of us still going through the evolution and ascension process must clear out our Eighth chakra once it opens up, because that chakra is the final repository for all karma. The fact that we are evolving and becoming more sentient (feeling) is "writ large" in the Crystal.

Crystals arrive with their psychic powers—clairvoyance, astral travel, telepathy, healing abilities, and so on—already intact. No wonder they are late talkers: Why speak if you've come fully equipped with high-speed telepathic abilities? Why talk when you can telepathically text? Most of us struggle to keep up with technology, but as the Crystals have already demonstrated, we are upgrading to actually *become* the new technology. Although Crystal children have many of the same attributes as Indigos, such as sensitivities to processed foods and a highly spiritual nature, they have many special characteristics all their own. Here are a few of them:

- Extremely vulnerable.
- Prefer being alone; dislike being in large groups.
- Empathic.
- Thrive on a vegan, organic diet; show sensitivity to elements that interfere with the pineal gland (Third-Eye chakra), such as fluoride.
- Communicate with animals.
- Often interested in crystals and gemstones.
- Often have large eyes that seem to penetrate the soul.
- Seemingly stoic; rarely show strong displays of emotion.
- Electrical gadgets sometimes malfunction around them.
- Creative and musical.
- Suffer from depression if they are in a disruptive environment.
- Able to heal themselves and others.
- Undergoing the beginning stages of "junk" DNA activation, which will enable all of us to connect to the psychic realms.

The Rainbow Children

The next spiritual upgrade can be found in the Rainbow children, sometimes also referred to as the Crystal Rainbow children. These children have illuminated auras that pull in the entire color spectrum, just as the auras of the Crystal children do, but with a much stronger intensity. When a Rainbow decides to incarnate on Earth he or she usually chooses more evolved parents, such as Indigos and Crystals. Rainbows are the neophytes; they are here to help our planet reseed itself with advanced spiritual beings who will be able to function in the many galactic communities beyond the Milky Way. Rainbows have fully functioning extrasensory abilities that correspond to the physical senses, giving them an almost preternatural ability to understand even the impenetrable mysteries of the universe. Rainbows are not attached to material things, and certainly they do not gauge their identities by what they own; rather, they know that they can have all they want and need by simply manifesting their desires. Rainbows identify with the creative vibes of the universe that are connected to the selfless collective consciousness rather than the selfish ego.

> Rainbows are here to help our planet reseed itself with advanced spiritual beings who will be able to function in the many galactic communities beyond the Milky Way.

Telepathy and remote viewing come naturally to these new *Homo sentients* because they come into their incarnation with a fully open Eighth chakra. Most likely their grandparents or great-grandparents were the last of the *Homo sapiens* species before the energy shift that fully activated their seventh chakra, the Crown chakra—the last milestone of human awareness that finally integrates the first six chakras. Rainbows also are born more crystal-based than carbon-based, meaning that the additional strands of their DNA that code to light frequency are already activated, thereby making their psychic senses much more apparent. Rainbow children function similarly to the Perfects, the original beings that had their first Earthly incarnation on the continent of

Atlantis. Like these primeval Atlanteans, Rainbows enjoy perfect balance between their male and female side, their yin and yang. Their many gifts include thought manifestation and instantaneous healing. Because Rainbow children are so highly advanced psychically, they need to be in families that are responsible with their abilities and won't exploit them. Fortunately Rainbows usually choose only well-adjusted families when they incarnate, as dysfunctional families do not resonate with their sensitive energy.

The Rainbow generation will be the last to be relegated to the material world's time-space paradigm because of their innate ability to access the higher spiritual chakras. Beginning with their already opened Eighth chakra, the rest will unfold like flowers, including the ninth (the soul's blueprint), the 10th (divine creativity merging the yin and yang, masculine and feminine energies), the 11th (time travel and instantaneous perception), and, finally, the 12th (advanced spiritual skills beyond the cosmos and connecting into the Divine).

Here are a few more characteristics of the Rainbow children:

※ Born after 2000, the largest influx arriving between 2011 and 2030.

※ Likely to have Indigo or Crystal parents.

※ Healing abilities.

※ Very creative; tune in easily to the vibrations from color.

※ Sensitive and loving.

※ Born with a fully functioning pineal gland; open to their extrasensory senses and telepathic.

※ Require a light, organic diet free from additives and pesticides; foods that are too difficult to digest will lower their frequency.

※ Easily frustrated with structured systems that don't encourage creativity.

※ Need very little sleep.

※ Like to work alone.

⚘ Usually have large penetrating eyes and sometimes a very high forehead to accommodate their changing brains.

⚘ Females are prone to have fine hair whereas males have a tendency to have sparse hair and prematurely receding hairlines.

These amazing people—the Indigo, Crystal, and Rainbow children—are the new lightworkers who are here to help the rest of the inhabitants of planet Earth make the transition into the higher dimensions of consciousness and finally evolve into the advanced beings we were designed to be. Those of us who are not Indigos, Crystals, or Rainbows will not be left behind, nor will we have to go through this process alone. By reading this book you have taken that first step in finding out what lies ahead for the care of your evolved body, mind, and spirit. Your inner sense is drawing you to this material to help you further your advancement into a world of spirit and energy while growing less concerned with the ephemeral material world.

> These amazing people are here to help us make the transition into the higher dimensions of consciousness and finally evolve into the advanced beings we were designed to be.

Because we are all evolving, you may be able to relate to some or even all of the characteristics of these children. This is because the subtle energies coming in are gradually tuning you to the new frequencies necessary for transition into and survival in a world of spiritual energy. Those who are *not* open, however, and who refuse to let go of the old, structured ways of three-dimensional consciousness may experience a more difficult transition. Survival of the fittest has always been the way of evolution, and here it is no different: Those who can't stay with the program may find the world of limited consciousness to be a three-dimensional box with the lid tightly shut, stifling and suffocating them.

To find out how this glorious process of transformation and rebirth will take place, read on. Don't be one of those who are left behind!

CHAPTER 2

Quickening: Signs of New Life

In pregnancy, *quickening* is the term used to describe the time when a woman first becomes aware of the signs of new life inside her. I use the term here to refer to the time when we open up to the fourth dimension (otherwise known as the astral plane) and begin to notice our extrasensory abilities, which are just becoming more prominent. Those little feelings inside of you—those still, small voices of intuition—kick in to become stronger feelings of *knowing*, which you will eventually learn to recognize and honor as truth. During the Quickening phase of your evolution you will experience such phenomena as déjà vu and parallel lives more regularly and more often. Dreaming, daydreaming, imagination, intuition, magick, psychic ability, and creativity are all ignited in the fourth dimension as well.

We perceive the physical world through the five physical senses, but we perceive the unseen world through the five subtle senses. The

We perceive the unseen world through the five subtle senses.

higher self or super-conscious mind exists on a higher plane beyond that of the physical body; it is what directs dreams, intuitions, and premonitions to the subconscious mind. The subconscious mind then acts as a storage file for all the spiritual perceptions and vibrations you pick up with your subtle senses, and also the information received by the conscious mind. It is through these subconscious communiqués from your subtle senses that abilities such as psychic powers and intuition are realized and mastered. In order to access their psychic abilities, people have tried to tap into the subconscious mind through various techniques—for example, meditation, drugs, and hypnosis. Now, however, experiencing our subtle senses will be a natural outgrowth of our evolution. We will finally see all of our experiences as a singular, connected whole. This amazing experience is akin to tasting the final product of a perfectly baked and beautifully iced cake when, previously, all you have ever eaten are eggs, butter, flour, and sugar by themselves.

The speed at which we ascend in this evolutionary process won't just affect how we think and act; even our sense of time itself will be altered. Many of us don't even realize that we are participating in the fourth and even the fifth dimension of consciousness because we have not yet broken ourselves of the limiting habit of counting days, hours, and minutes. We only notice that time seems different somehow. The etheric or astral body resides in the fourth dimension and sees the past, present, and future as one. As you might have already intuited, compartmentalizing the past, present, and future; time and space; cause and effect—and the attendant feeling of separateness this engenders—is no longer viable in the fourth dimension. This is because we begin to experience collective consciousness as opposed to just looking for ego-based outcomes.

Indeed, as of this writing, many people are complaining that that time seems to be speeding up. As I explained in the previous chapter, as we become more crystal-based, we are pulling in a faster, lighter frequency due to Earth's position in the galaxy, and this can sometimes cause a kind of mental "short circuiting" and sense of disorientation. Thus, as we make that shift from third-dimensional consciousness to higher-dimensional consciousness, time will no longer be experienced in a linear fashion. Eventually, time and space will join together, creating a singular entity called *space-time*. Time is relative, and this is never more apparent than when one remains in limited, three-dimensional consciousness—which, of course, consigns one to just 24 hours in a day. Most people would agree that time seems to be flying by—unless of course you are stuck on a bad date or put on hold waiting for the next available customer representative to help you. In all seriousness, though, there is a general consensus that our days seem to be moving toward some unknown end rather quickly.

At this stage it is also common to be running two or more consciousness programs at the same time—again, because you are making that shift into one, unified frequency. This happens when your energetic spirit essence expands beyond its current experience and slips into another reality that is either from a distant coordinate in space (the past) or from a projected thought manifestation (the future). This is similar to sitting in front of your computer screen and using one program while several other programs are running in the background. As most of us are well aware, this can slow things down quite a bit. This is why some people complain of feeling fatigued and disoriented during the Quickening phase.

> Eventually, time and space will join together, creating a singular entity called space-time.

During the Quickening phase it is also not uncommon to have days when you feel "out there" and basically lost in space, so be prepared for that. Drifting off and daydreaming beyond the third dimension can be a confusing and unsettling experience, because the fourth dimension is made up of several different planes of consciousness. Parallel lives and sudden transitions into other states of existence can also account for the confusion that is often experienced during this phase. We usually can't handle parallel life episodes safely and comfortably unless and until we master the skill of "defragging" our consciousness as we ascend through the fourth dimension. Defragging (defragmentation) is a process that reduces the amount of fragmentation in file systems in computers; in the realm of consciousness, it helps reduce the amount of frequency interference from other incarnations. Letting go of all attachments to unnecessary thoughts, beliefs, fears, and linear modes of perception that include terms such as *past* and *future* begins the defragmentation process. This allows us to expand our awareness and realize that we are multisensory and multidimensional beings. Eventually we can experience what it feels like to move from matter into quantum reality. Time and space become interchangeable, and we see that there is no longer any separateness in the universe.

We are multisensory and multidimensional beings.

As you ascend and evolve you will need to address *all* of your experiences in *all* of your incarnations. This will involve looking through the "files" of your other lives and becoming acquainted with their contents in order to discover where certain energy patterns are still residing in your consciousness. When you live through an emotionally disturbing event, you retain an energy imprint of its memory in your consciousness. Unresolved relationships, fears, and emotions will hold sway over your present life experience until you clear them out. (This is usually done by transforming their energy frequency into a more refined vibration that is free from interference and "static." I'll describe this process in greater detail in the next chapter.) Healing modalities such as past life regression and Reiki can help transmute fear-based energy blockages into a lighter frequency that resonates to the love-based vibrations. The vibrations of other life experiences will continue to resonate throughout the universe the way that an echo resounds in a canyon. The energy that is sourced from you will eternally shift, change, combine, reverberate, and become part of the collective consciousness. This is all just another way of saying that repetitive patterns in your life are usually caused by your own energy returning to the source from whence it came.

The Lower Astral Level

The lower level of the fourth dimension, the lower astral level, harbors all of our thoughts that were created out of fear. It is the cosmic spam folder that captures all of the negative thoughts and energies that splinter off and become fragmented when we are angry, jealous, or fearful. This is the place we visit when we have nightmares; some people even feel that it is actually a form of hell. Facing our own demons—which, again, we more or less create—can help us get past these fears and false beliefs and move closer to the light. This level of the fourth dimension also holds all of the thoughts that eventually give rise to our future experiences. When you worry about something and assume a probable outcome—both of which are ways of projecting into the future—you are actually setting yourself up to experience those very scenarios while preventing yourself from creating a better outcome. You have the power to determine the outcome of any given situation. That's right: *You* create your reality. Don't get me wrong—planning for the future is fine, but creating scenarios built upon fear will often leave you vulnerable to an *ascension virus*, which will shut you down, block your extrasensory senses, and keep you trapped inside the three-dimensional box.

By way of an example, I sometimes notice that I feel a little "off" on certain days, particularly when I have been guilty of worrying. My physical body usually tells me that my vibration is being compromised by my fear-based emotions; when this happens, my personal warning system, my sinuses, begin to ache. I know enough about the risks inherent in the practice of worrying to address the problem head-on before it causes my energy to crash completely. I know to immediately shift myself back into the Now, where I can center myself and put a stop to any negative outcomes. As you become more acquainted with your emerging subtle body, you will be able to identify your own personal cautionary signals that alert you to low vibrations coming into your system, in much the same way that a smoke detector lets you know that there is a fire nearby.

> Creating scenarios built upon fear will often leave you vulnerable to an ascension virus.

Similarly, I can immediately tell when I am running more than one consciousness program (parallel lives) at the same time because I'm usually unable to organize my thoughts or manage my time. Concentration becomes more difficult, and a kind of cosmic ADD (attention deficit disorder) sets in. This is similar to what happens when your car drifts into another lane of traffic because you are not paying attention or are nodding off. Clearly this can cause big problems if you don't snap back into the moment! Energetically speaking, the result can be "accidents" such as arguments, meltdowns, anxiety attacks, phobic thoughts, and other unwanted feelings. This can wreak emotional havoc on you and others, and diminish your overall energy. Imagine getting angry at someone because of an imprinted emotion from a distant life experience that you shared and haven't dealt with! Much of how we react to things is caused by excess painful emotional energy imprints that are still linked to our spirit or energy essence. But the good news is that knowing about the potential pitfalls can help you avoid these kinds of problems altogether.

The Etheric Level

The upper level of the fourth dimension, the etheric level, is where we go during out-of-body experiences and visits with deceased loved ones and others who are waiting to ascend. The first time you experience this during the Quickening stage can be pretty scary if you don't know what's going on. You may feel certain you are dreaming or even going crazy. This level is also a very magickal place where the thought-forms of fairies, gnomes, salamanders, elves, and spirit guides reside. Think of it as the Greenwich Village or Chelsea of the fourth dimension! This is the home of the ether waves: the cosmic, creative, magickal energy zone where our wishes materialize in an instant and where our thoughts become a created reality. Shamans and energy workers who have mastered this plane are savvy enough to recognize the benefits of working with the magickal energy beings that reside there. Once you shift into the new frequency, you, too, will be able to easily access this realm and its helpful residents.

The Mental Level

The mental level of the fourth dimension is where our psychic abilities are amplified, allowing us to connect with each other telepathically and psychically. It is where we learn to master our thoughts and project ourselves psychically. It is sort of like our psychic networking hub. All of our psychic and spiritual abilities function in the mental plane as a means of creating reality. This is the canvas of the conscious mind from which we create physical reality itself. Collective consciousness generates enough psychic force at this level to bring about changes in the lower third dimension of weight and mass. For this reason, you will need to master the skill of keeping your thoughts pure and free from the trappings of the material world. Vices such as greed, jealousy, lust, and other negative, fear-based emotions that are second nature to *Homo sapiens* will not vibrate well in this dimension, because these frequencies are too low to sustain themselves there. The lower vibrations from negative thoughts are distorted with energy blockages from painful thoughts and emotions. Because they are too heavy to ascend, these vibrations usually remain in the lower astral level, which some call hell or the underworld.

> All of our psychic and spiritual abilities function in the mental plane as a means of creating reality.

Our evolution requires us to become very familiar with our energetic makeup, which will involve a brief discussion of our chakra centers, the "master spark plugs" that connect us to the world of energy. Our evolution into becoming more psychic, extrasensory beings comes about to the extent that these energy centers respond to the incoming shift in energy.

The Chakra System

Chakras (Sanskrit for "wheels") are energy-sensitive vortices located in specific areas of the body. Basically, they are your energy control centers. When they are spinning freely they help your physical body function optimally. They also help alert you to energy imbalances, usually by manifesting as disease or illness. As you become more *Homo sentient*, these centers will open up to their full extrasensory capabilities. Once you open up psychically you will be able to sense energy coming from the thoughts and intentions of others; energy imprints left on people, places, and things; vibrations from the foods you eat; and the general vibration emanating from the collective consciousness. Imagine these chakra centers as points of confluence or gateways residing on your energy grid, regulating and adjusting the flow of energy as you ascend and evolve. Although most of the chakras are actually located on the hands and feet (something that many people don't know), we take special note of the seven main chakras that begin at the base of the spine and end at the crown of the head. These chakras are also located in the ethereal body and express spiritual energy on the physical plane. As we shift into the next phase of our evolution, additional chakras will appear and open up in order to accommodate our evolving spiritual and physical form.

> The subtle or energetic body has to be treated and cared for just as the physical body does.

Many of us fail to pay attention to these very sensitive energy zones because we have been conditioned to recognize only the tenets of Western medicine, which deals primarily with the physical body. Eastern medicine, on the other hand, has always been aware of the importance of the energetic body. It also acknowledges how exposure to energy first affects the light body before manifesting into a physical condition. Ancient physicians knew that the subtle or energetic body—the light body—had to be treated and cared for just as the physical body did. Eastern medicine has always recognized that disturbances, imbalances, and impediments in the flow of energy within the chakras have a symbiotic relationship with disturbances in the physical body as well as the life and circumstances of an individual.

As we become more sentient and extrasensory, we will become much more aware of how our chakras are connecting us to this influx of higher, transformative frequencies. These frequencies resonate with our chakras and fully activate the five spiritual body senses that correspond to our five physical body senses. This will result in our becoming more intuitive and more psychic—in other words, light-based rather than carbon-based. Interestingly, even our technology is becoming more intuitive. As of this writing, voice recognition devices, sensory crash avoidance features in cars, and even a mirror that can read and decipher your emotions are just some of the inventions that will dovetail quite nicely with our own "upgrades." With all this in mind, let's take a look at the main chakra system and see which psychic sense corresponds to each one of these energy centers, and what you can do to help maintain these new, advanced ways of perceiving.

Your first chakra, called the **Root chakra,** is located at the base of the spine near the coccyx. This chakra opens downward and relates to the energy of physical grounding (connecting or "grounding" the body to earth energies) and survival. Because this chakra connects you to the physical world, it is also associated with your relationship to time and how you perceive it. This chakra is your primal memory center; it holds all of your early childhood memories and, therefore, your attitude regarding security.

As this chakra opens to its full capacity, it will activate your psychic sense of smell. You probably never realized that you even had this amazing psychic sense, as most schools of thought don't bother to recognize it at all. Look at how connected animals are to their basic instincts when it comes to survival; much of this is based on their sense of smell. For us it is no different. Believe it or not, you function primarily from this chakra until about the age of 7. Currently the layer of your subtle body that holds your emotions will link various scents to corresponding memories, which will hold either a good impression or a bad impression. When your psychic sense of smell (*clairscent,* sometimes called *clairolfactory*) opens up, you will be able to actually *smell* energy. "Something's rotten in the state of Demark," "The whole thing stinks," "I smell change in the air"—all of these phrases point to how we can sense the quality of the energy of a given person or situation. Like an animal that can detect cancer and even the scent of impending death, eventually you'll be able to use your psychic smell to detect illness or disease in the body, as well as the "scent" of danger.

How will you know that your psychic sense of smell is activated, and how will you be able to tell the difference between clairscent and your physical sense of smell? You will know that your psychic sense of smell is activated when you smell inexplicable odors that aren't apparent to others. You will recognize foul smells as indicative of negative energy or disease, or of someone or something that is not good for you. A client of mine once told me that every time her ex-husband was about to call her, she would smell the scent of cucumbers. It turns out that her ex was a very unfeeling person, and she was detecting—quite unknowingly—the scent of something familiar to her that her subconscious related to his cold personality. She was actually psychically smelling and even tasting his energy before the phone rang. You will be able to smell the energy of every single situation and discern whether it is pleasant or foul, thereby enabling you to have full psychic awareness of anything that comes your way. The scent of roses is commonly detected in the presence of positive energy. It is often present when we connect to the higher realms because its high vibration resonates with the higher frequencies. You may smell the scent of roses when connecting with a higher being or a deceased loved one. Is it any wonder, then, that we associate roses with love? Psychics who go on paranormal investigations will sometimes pick up a strong scent or odor as well. This enables them to piece together information about the locale. The scent of sulfur, for example, is commonly experienced in these situations, particularly when the psychic is dealing with very low vibrations that are associated with negative, demonic energy and/or trapped energy, such as what is often found in hauntings.

Your second chakra, the **Sacral chakra**, is located just beneath the navel and opens forward. It is associated with sexuality, sensuality, and pleasure. This is the chakra where you balance sex, money, and emotions.

Any unexpressed or repressed emotions, especially those stemming from childhood, are found here. The second chakra finds expression in your creations, your children, your passions, and the abundance that you let into your life. When this chakra is not spinning properly, control issues, sexual hang-ups, and emotional drama are usually the result. This chakra is also associated with attachments and addictions. Because we must learn how to detach from the concerns and needs of the physical world, this chakra plays a big part in our evolution.

The psychic sense of this chakra is *clairgustation*, or psychic taste, which is analogous to your basic tastes and proclivities, your likes and dislikes. Is life generally sweet, or are you bitter about what has happened to you? If something or someone "left a bad taste in your mouth," chances are it was a negative situation that left behind a negative energy imprint. The taste of energy is often experienced as a tingly tongue, dry mouth, excessive salivation, or even a familiar taste that triggers an associated memory. The more aware and highly evolved we are, the more familiar the various tastes from different energies will become.

You will also be able to tell whether something you are eating is good or bad for you by the "taste" of its energy, regardless of how it actually tastes. Imagine eating a piece of cake that tastes great on a superficial level, but tastes terrible on an energetic level. This is your spirit telling you that this particular food probably isn't the best choice. As we evolve into lighter beings, we will probably need to start counting our units of energy not by calories, but by vibrational frequency. Who knows? Maybe Weight Watchers will eventually become *Wattage* Watchers.

The third chakra, the **Solar Plexus chakra**, is located near the navel. The energy from this chakra flows upward and shifts the energy from the earthly, primal connections of the lower chakras to the higher group of spiritual chakras. The third chakra relates to personal power, destiny, and psychic ability. Once this chakra is fully activated it will act as a bridge between the higher and lower chakras so that we can merge the physical with the spiritual and learn to surrender the ego. The psychic sense associated with this chakra is intuition or insight. Once this chakra is open and activated, the potential range of psychic perception is phenomenal. Just as your eyes sense light and dark, the psychic sense of insight recognizes both light (good) and dark (bad) energy. Often, this kind of insight registers as a "gut feeling"—not surprising, really, given the location of this chakra. We may also feel chills or some other physical sensation that clues us in to the character of the energy we're picking up on. These feelings are often collectively referred to as *clairsentience*, French for "clear feeling." Clairsentience and precognition both originate from this chakra, and they work together to give you an extended extrasensory representation—a panoramic snapshot, if you will—of the energy around you. Once your third chakra is sufficiently evolved, you will be able to clearly feel the energy around you. Vibrations will register in your solar plexus as a distinct gut feeling or an inner knowing. Believe me when I say that when this psychic sense kicks in, you'll know it!

> The psychic sense of insight recognizes both light (good) and dark (bad) energy.

As we ascend and evolve, the veil between us and the three-dimensional world of illusion and false reality will become more and more transparent. The agendas and motives of others will suddenly become crystal clear. This cuts both ways: Although we're all evolving at different rates, most people will eventually be able to discern your energy, too. We are all required to be authentic, not only with ourselves but also with others. Speaking more practically and concretely, a fully activated and developed third chakra will certainly make it more difficult for people to keep secrets from one another, so you can imagine the impact this will have on all relationships, both personal and professional. Eventually you will only need to touch an object belonging to someone or simply be around a person to discern his or her true intentions.

How will you know when this particular psychic sense is at work? You probably have experienced psychic impressions throughout your life, but dismissed these feelings as anomalies or coincidences. Perhaps you've had that adrenaline rush that comes from a near-miss accident or mishap. You probably felt a rush of energy and may have had a slight ringing or clogged sensation in your ears. You were actually sensing the energy readout for "danger." Feeling energy as a rush or wave after having just narrowly escaped danger or disaster is a pretty basic feeling that most people are familiar with; after all, it's part of the fight-or-flight instinct common to all animals. When you are fully *Homo sentient* you will be able to sense these sorts of things *far* in advance. Far from being only a negative experience, you will also be able to feel the energy of anticipation when something good is about to happen. You will feel an excited tingle of energy as you sense the arrival of good news before you actually hear it. Happiness has a high frequency that is discernible even to the novice. That said, before you can ascertain if your psychic senses are activated, you will first need to acknowledge and fully "own" them. This is all a part of adjusting your mind and body to accommodate living in a world that is primarily composed of and informed by energy. You can start to prepare yourself for this simply by *using* those senses just as you do your physical senses. We'll get into that more in later chapters.

The fourth chakra, also called the **Seat of the Soul**, is located near—you guessed it—the heart, and opens forward. This is the energy center where our perceptions are transformed into emotions. It is our center of unconditional love and the seat of all emotional memory. Emotions are our way of communicating what we are feeling on an energetic level, which we then demonstrate on a physical level through our words and deeds. When this energy center is fully opened and evolved, psychic touch (*psychometry*) and innate healing abilities kick in. Psychometry is the practice of touching an object in order to read its history or that of its owner(s). The highest, most advanced form of psychic touch is healing touch, which enables us to transmit the highest-frequency vibrations (those associated with love and compassion) to others. We all possess the power of healing touch because we are hardwired for it. Our evolution will merely make us more aware of this natural ability to diagnose health problems and even heal. Many of you have probably already experienced a psychic connection to your own health or that of a spouse, close friend, or family member. Perhaps you were able to sense that something was wrong before there was even a presenting health problem. Many patients

We all possess the power of healing touch.

in hospitals show improved breathing and heart rate when a loved one or caring person holds their hand or strokes their forehead. That is healing touch in action. Medical intuitives, Reiki practitioners, and shamans all know how to channel their energy and tap into the human aura or energy field to fix any vibrational imbalances that manifest as physical ailments. Even inherited diseases and disorders resulting from past karma will be treated and eventually cured by getting to the root cause, which is usually a blockage, misfire, or corruption somewhere in the subtle body as a result of a negative emotional impact or trauma. In Chapter 3 I will delve more deeply into diseases and conditions that often result from past life trauma.

The fifth chakra actually comprises two separate chakras—a larger one located between the depression in the neck and the larynx, and another, smaller chakra that opens to the back. Because these chakras are so close together, they are integrated into one as the **Throat chakra.** This chakra is the center of communication, inspiration, and manifestation. As many mystics already know, the spoken word has a great deal of manifestation power, particularly if a word is repeated over and over again. As we evolve, the Throat chakra expands and activates our psychic sense of hearing, called *clairaudience*. Clairaudience is essentially the energetic body's ability to hear in a paranormal manner. It occurs when you tune in to a frequency beyond the physical world and receive messages. Channeling is one way that this extrasensory sense of the spirit is often displayed, but you don't have to be deemed a psychic or medium to have this ability; everyone possesses it. All you need to do is learn to listen to the messages from the universe the same way a baby learns language by listening to the spoken word. Many people think that clairaudience is only limited to receiving messages from the dead. Actually it is listening to your spirit's built-in GPS and receiving guidance from Ascended Masters, interdimensional beings, guides, and, well, pretty much the whole universe.

A word of caution: Although clairaudience can easily be integrated into your daily life, it is still a very misunderstood ability. A very psychic woman I used to know once went to the doctor because she was experiencing anxiety related to a family situation. At one point he asked her if she ever heard voices in her head, and when she quite truthfully answered that she often tuned in to messages from beyond, he actually took steps to have her committed. This just goes to show you how the language of the spirit is often misunderstood. What medical doctors can't understand they choose to ignore, medicate, or silence. Clearly the transition from science to spirit has still not yet been perfected.

The sixth chakra is located right above the bridge of the nose in the center of the forehead, and opens to the front. Commonly referred to as the **Third Eye** or **Clairvoyant Eye**, this chakra is considered to be the seat of our higher mental powers, where our ESP links into the physical body via the *pineal gland*, a tiny, pine cone–shaped gland situated deep in the brain. (I will discuss the remarkable features of the pineal gland in greater depth Chapter 4, as it is integral to our evolution.) In some cultures this chakra is represented by a mark or small jewel on the forehead. The psychic abilities associated with this chakra are telepathy, astral travel, connecting to parallel lives, and *clairvoyance*, also known as psychic sight or the sight of the soul. Clairvoyance is what comes into play during *remote viewing*, which is the ability to gather information about an otherwise-unknown locale (called a "target"). Governments have used clairvoyant remote viewers for top-secret missions and spying. Not surprisingly, this chakra seems to be the one most referenced when describing psychic abilities and ESP.

How do you tell the difference between clairvoyant impressions and mere imagination? The line between the two is not as defined as you would think. The imagination is where thought-forms are created, and, if given enough of a push by the energy of desire, they can eventually materialize into third-dimensional reality. To confirm whether your clairvoyant impressions are for real, look for corresponding signals from your other chakras and newly evolved extrasensory senses. Are you getting a visual accompanied by an energy rush or chills as confirmation? Or perhaps you are getting confirmation from an inner voice. Also, be aware of what you are feeling when you receive a clairvoyant image or impression, and whether you are feeling a particular emotion or emotions at the time. It may also help to remember that clairvoyance is simply a visual representation of the energy you are sensing.

Did you know that we are all born clairvoyant? In the past most people scoffed at the idea of extrasensory senses, and therefore the development and use of our innate psychic senses was not encouraged or even addressed. The process of evolution will awaken *everyone's* clairvoyant eye, making it natural for us to see through and beyond the material world. I think it is safe to say that we are naturally pre-programmed to be psychic. Telepathy, a close relative of clairvoyance, is the ability to send or receive thoughts, images, feelings, or impressions from one person to another without the use of the five physical senses. Freud thought that telepathy was a regressive, primitive faculty that had been lost in the course of evolution, but could still manifest itself under certain conditions. He was wrong about it being regressive: Eventually this is how we will all communicate, focusing and sending out thoughts, which are then picked up by the intended recipient(s). When it is fully expanded, the sixth chakra will also enable us to experience astral travel to other dimensions of consciousness as well as out-of-body experiences. Eventually we will be able to visit other lives we have been a part of as well as those lives we have purposefully created for ourselves via our own creative thoughts.

We are all born clairvoyant.

The seventh chakra, also known as the **Crown chakra**, is located at the middle of the top of the head, and opens upward. This chakra is linked to the *pituitary gland*, also called the master gland. The pituitary gland works closely with the pineal gland in order to give us full extrasensory faculties. In religious paintings the Crown chakra is often represented as a halo, indicating where personal energy connects to the Divine energy of the universe. Once your Crown chakra is fully open, any remaining blockages in the lower six chakras will dissolve. Before the Crown chakra can function at its best, however, all the other chakra energy centers must be refined and balanced. The extrasensory sense associated with this chakra is Divine knowing. As we evolve, our ability to sense and manipulate energy from the universal Source will become more and more natural. The Crown area is the portal connecting us with the ever-increasing frequencies of the expanding universe. As you grow more accustomed to working with all of your chakra centers, it will become much easier for you to open and close this chakra at will, thereby allowing only the right kind of energy into your system. Opening the Crown chakra to the wrong vibrations—or, conversely, not closing it completely at critical times—may leave you vulnerable to an influx of negative energy in the form of a cosmic virus.

How can you tell when your Crown chakra is activated? Believe it or not, noticeable headaches, particularly across the top of the head, may be the first sign. Some people may also find that they have a tendency to have episodes of "spacing out" momentarily; this is a side effect of taking in more energy. If this happens to you, keep reminding yourself that we all live in a world of energy and that the physical world is only a creation of our thoughts. As we move into the next phase of our evolution, we'll become more accustomed to what energy feels like as our extrasensory system activates.

Our evolution isn't limited to the seven chakras I've discussed. We are also prewired to activate additional chakra centers as our evolution unfolds.

The **Eighth chakra**, also called the Soul Star chakra, which will be activated once our evolutionary shift is complete, sits about an arm's length above the Crown chakra. It is the energy center of Divine love, spiritual compassion, and spiritual selflessness. This chakra holds the record of the lessons our soul has agreed to, as well as our soul contracts. These contracts are made with other souls and the Divine in order to further our spiritual growth and transformation. This chakra also connects into the Akashic Record, the master recording of all of your incarnations, including the ones that have not yet manifested. Your contract with the Divine is always accessible through this chakra center. The Eighth chakra also connects with your electromagnetic field (aura), but there are no shadow emotions or imbalances in this chakra because it is so closely connected with the Divine.

We can expect the activation of the **Diaphragm chakra**, sometimes called the **Buddha Belly chakra**, because this is where we store emotional memory. Remember that emotional memory needs to be rebalanced because the lower vibrations associated with negative emotions can't resonate with the higher frequencies of the advanced dimensions. Have you ever noticed that stressed-out people tend to have larger bellies? This is usually associated with excess cortisol, the stress hormone produced by the adrenal glands, which are linked to this chakra. With continual stress, the cortisol causes fat to be stored around the midsection. The transformative process can itself be a source of stress, as we dredge up old emotions and let go of things we once thought we needed. You can see how feeling unsafe or ungrounded (think: fight-or-flight reaction) causes stress, which releases cortisol. A fully open and active Diaphragm chakra will help you process your emotional energy and keep your system clear.

> Intention is the force behind what we create with our thoughts.

We also have the **Thymus chakra**, which is located in the upper chest area just above and to the right of the Heart chakra. This chakra is vital to our psychic evolution: It will help us regulate our newly activated psychic abilities because this is where we become aware of our intentions. Intention is the force behind what we create with our thoughts, and it is an important part of the evolution of our activated psychic senses. (Again, you must always be responsible with your advanced capabilities, because the wrong intentions can wreak havoc in your life and the lives of others.) When this chakra is activated initially, it is common to experience bouts of *tachycardia*, or elevated heart rate. This seems to occur mostly at night, around bedtime, when we review our day and feel or process our own energy and the energetic intentions coming from others.

Hopefully you now have a better understanding of the importance of the chakra system, and particularly how it relates to one's advanced psychic abilities. The chakras have a direct bearing on the physical body—the shell, if you will, that houses your energy body. Any upsets in the main energy grid will show up as blocked psychic abilities and physical ailments. The new anatomy of the *Homo sentient* encompasses more than just the physical; the skin, bones, and organs of the body. It is the psychic connection to the universe that will help keep you "online" and on track in your evolution. The chakras I've discussed here are the ones that have the most direct connection to and impact on the physical body, and are the ones responsible for helping you tune in to your psychic senses so that you can transition more easily into the frequencies of the higher dimensions.

Ascension Depression

Now that you have a better understanding of how energy works, you will begin to realize how vibrations from repressed emotions, from the process of detaching from a solely material consciousness, and from fear-based feelings can all bring about a temporary condition known as *ascension depression*. Depression itself is certainly nothing new. We all know that it can be triggered by life-altering events or chemical imbalances in the brain due to genetics, diet, or drugs. What many people don't know, however, is that it is sometimes caused by inherited karma from a previous incarnation. I call it ascension depression because it is directly tied to our evolution—ascension—as a species.

This particular type of depression usually arises because of a blocked Root chakra, which in turn affects the energy in the other chakra centers. It is similar to how a car sputters and misfires if the spark plugs aren't gapped correctly. The Root chakra, the energy center located at the base of the spine, affects how grounded and secure you feel in the material world. It is the place where you store childhood memories, your contributions to the collective unconscious, your memories from other incarnations, and your connection to the physical world. This chakra is also where we pull in Kundalini energy, the primordial cosmic energy present in every single person. (*Kundalini* is a Sanskrit word meaning "coiled power" or "serpent power.") Kundalini awakening is a very powerful thing indeed, and sometimes the brain can't adapt quickly

Kundalini energy can help clear your chakra centers of stagnant and/or negative energy.

enough to the intensity of this surge of energy. Ascension depression can often result from the inevitable letdown after the energy recedes; in fact, we'll likely feel this way each time until we can learn to maintain a comfortable, even flow of energy throughout our chakra system. Once it is released, however, this Kundalini energy greatly aids our extrasensory and psychic awakening. Kundalini energy can help clear your chakra centers of stagnant and/or negative energy, thereby allowing each chakra to operate at its optimum capacity. This improves the overall condition of the aura and jacks up your frequency/vibration, which in turn opens up your psychic abilities.

In addition to being a possible tipping point for cosmic depression, this chakra also contains the eight primary cells that contain within them all the secrets of your creation—your DNA. Here you will find the only cells in your body that do not change throughout your lifetime. Each cell in this chakra holds the keys to your original consciousness and genetic code. In a later chapter I will get into how additional strands of our DNA are going to be activated, thereby putting us more in line with our true ancestry.

We've already discussed how we are essentially a trinity consisting of body, mind, and spirit. Our ascension or evolution will connect us more securely with our spirit or energy body. When these three components eventually merge into one, we will recognize with great clarity that security doesn't come from material things such as homes, cars, jobs, or money. Our security will come from our ability to stay in the moment, control our thoughts, focus on what we need, maintain our energy, and, ultimately, manifest and create the life we

We are essentially a trinity consisting of body, mind, and spirit.

desire. The dizzying speed at which these changes occur can leave us feeling a bit out of control and directionless at times—another contributor to this depression.

Interestingly, weight gain is another common "side effect" of our evolution. This is because the new frequency coming in is very strong, and the body often creates excess body fat to act as an insulator. Some of this weight gain can be due to excess water weight, too, as becoming more psychically attuned rebalances the water in the body. This is because water is a wonderfully efficient conductor of electricity. If this happens to you, know that your body will eventually find its balance.

As you evolve, your physical body will become increasingly sensitive to what you pick up with your advanced extrasensory senses. This can feel similar to going to the movies and putting on 3D glasses for the very first time. The strangeness of it all can be very confusing, which can contribute to depression. As well, once you start to realize that the structured systems that you once bought into have let you down, you will no longer feel as safe as you once did. This is because the more evolved you are, spiritually speaking, the less enthused you will feel about any organization or relationship that stifles and endeavors to control you through the use of fear. Thus, you may go through a temporary period of disempowerment and depression as you detach, change, and align yourself to the new energy.

The biggest changes, however, will occur in our relationships. Most of this will be due to the fact that we won't all evolve at the same rate. For example, when you begin to open up spiritually, your vibration rises, so being around someone with a lower vibration can be boring and frustrating. *Your* values are shifting, but you may not find that everyone else feels or thinks as you do. Staying in a relationship in which one person is very materialistic—and, perhaps more importantly, not open to the changes going on in your life—can be quite a challenge. As you forge ahead and embrace your newfound abilities and sensibilities, you may feel remorse over the fact that you no longer share the same worldview or values with this person. Admittedly it can be depressing to leave even those relationships you know are not right for you, but try to see them as lessons and opportunities for growth. Always bless the person with good energy; avoid resentment, because that will lower your vibration and send you right back into the box with them. Know that moving outside of the box will bring you out into a whole new world to explore and vibrate to!

As you evolve and ascend you may find it difficult to express your feelings to others, and you may become discontent with situations that you once resonated to in your lower consciousness. If you don't feel free to express this discontentment, you may begin to repress your emotions and even turn your anger inward—yet another cause of depression. When we repress emotions we lower our overall vibration rate and start to pull in too much negative energy. This negative consciousness vibration is too heavy to coexist happily with the new, lighter frequencies coming in because it impedes the spinning of our chakras and compromises our perceptions. Indigo children often suffer from a form of ascension depression because they are misunderstood by society, relegated to classrooms for children with ADD, and given drugs such as Ritalin to suppress their boundless energy. As adults many become dependent on pharmaceuticals because of the ignorance surrounding their true gifts.

There also seems to be a bipolar type of ascension depression going around these days. People get depressed because they feel stuck, blocked, and repressed, and then they feel euphoric when they get a quick shot of that high-frequency energy. The highly creative Kundalini energy coming from the Root chakra sometimes triggers this kind of mania if there isn't enough grounding energy present. This imbalance sometimes presents as hallucinations (visual, olfactory, and auditory) and delusional thinking. The most important goal for a person with bipolar ascension depression is the proper balance and channeling of psychic and physical energy. *An important caveat for today's overmedicated society: Prescription drugs, particularly antidepressants and antipsychotics, can slow down and in some cases completely arrest the transformational process.* These drugs may appear to help initially, but they actually keep you from evolving naturally. In addition, the side effects are often more debilitating than the illness itself. All medications stress your liver, the bodily organ that is responsible for processing the vibrations of anger. Of course, you should always consult a medical professional regarding your health, but in my opinion most medications are not the answer to this particular kind of depression. In a later chapter I will discuss the new healing modalities that treat the body, mind, and spirit as one unit—a much better approach.

> Prescription drugs, particularly antidepressants and antipsychotics, can slow down and in some cases completely arrest the transformational process.

All of these changes, both positive and negative, are a part of a natural evolutionary process. If you do feel depressed, know that you now have the ability to heal yourself. There is likely no need for drugs that alter your mood, cause adverse side effects, and mess with your overall vibration and body chemistry. Of course, the pharmaceutical companies don't want you to know this. You might say that we are detoxing—purging our old beliefs, reinventing ourselves, and redefining our relationships with others and with the world in general. Again, you may feel some remorse as you let go of people, memories, and patterns that are no longer for your highest good. As with any detox there will likely be a period of withdrawal accompanied by restlessness and anxiety as a result of purging the darker and denser energy from your psyche. Even our lovely planet is detoxing. Strange weather patterns, earthquakes, volcanoes, and other natural disasters are Earth's way of cleansing herself from all of the negative vibrations in her aura (atmosphere) as a result of wars, greed, pollution, and other low vibrations from her inhabitants.

So what are we to do? Realize that every time we have a negative thought we can consciously remove it and replace it with something positive. I know what you're thinking: *Try telling that to someone who is having his or her home foreclosed, who is unemployed, or who is experiencing a significant loss.* The truth of the matter is everything we *think* we are losing is most likely something that is either unnecessary or bad for us. Focus on your Root chakra and pull in grounding energy as you release those heavy burdens you carry (most of which are based on the illusionary success markers of three-dimensional consciousness). You can create a better life if you embrace and align yourself with the new vibrations that will merge body, mind, and spirit, and blend past, present, and future into one complete stream of existence. Despite loss and pain, you will always evolve toward becoming whole by integrating every aspect of your being. Your depression may even serve the beneficial purpose of slowing you down enough to reevaluate the changes around you, adapt to a different routine, and allow for new changes to come about in your life. Those who refuse to let go of old beliefs and continue to resist the process of evolution will find themselves stuck, like a computer that has frozen. Their unease—*dis-ease*, really—with the new vibrations will very likely manifest as a disease, the severity of which will vary depending on the frequency of their thoughts. As our thought vibrations take precedence, we become more and more responsible for what we create for ourselves.

> As our thought vibrations take precedence, we become more and more responsible for what we create for ourselves.

Here are a few things that you can do to ease the depression that may come with your evolution:

- ❊ Get a deep tissue massage. Muscle can store memories of traumatic experiences, whether from this life or another one.

- ❊ Work on grounding your Root chakra. Visualize the color red in that area and begin to release any feelings of living in victim consciousness.

- ❊ St. John's Wort has been used for centuries as a medicinal herb that has mood-enhancing benefits. (Of course, always check with your physician before taking any herb or medication.)

- ❊ Sound therapy has been shown to increase the amount of dopamine and serotonin, which are neurotransmitters associated with happiness. The tone of "C" helps rebalance the Root chakra.

❋ Healing crystals such as lithium quartz, an antidepressant, are useful for calming negative emotions.

❋ Aromatherapy used in diffusion or as massage oils helps relieve stress and depression. Some suggestions: bergamot, cedarwood, chamomile, lavender, neroli, rose, and ylang-ylang.

Although some of this may sound a bit bleak, know that feeling depressed is *always* a natural response to the process of letting go. After all, we are still living in the physical world even as we are in the process of letting go of its limited and limiting beliefs. If this happens to you, relax: It is a normal phase to go through, and once you understand what it is you can easily move past its stifling affects.

In the next chapter we will turn our attention to what happens during the most difficult phase of your evolution, the Transition phase. But be comforted: With this difficulty comes much blessing and beauty.

CHAPTER 3

Transition: Shifting out of the Comfort Zone

Until now we have only touched on your true psychic capabilities during the Quickening phase of your evolution. Your latent psychic nature may have been evident to you only through occasional intuitive hunches, precognitive dreams, or feelings of "just knowing" without any left-brained, logical reason to back up your knowledge. As you evolve and begin to merge your physical nature with the frequency of your spiritual nature, your world takes on another dimension that allows you to more easily feel, sense, and interpret the energy around you. The Transition phase will bring about a full and complete experience of your awakened extrasensory senses.

The transition phase of childbirth is often the most difficult. This is when pain increases and things progress more rapidly, right before the "pushing" stage. There is no turning back at this point. Similarly, as you awaken and evolve into your psychic nature, you may at times feel

73

uncomfortable, strange, and even anxious given the new way in which you are experiencing the energy around you. But with heightened discomfort comes heightened awareness. The more adept you are at using your awakened extrasensory senses, the more vivid your existence will be. Colors appear brighter, smells more distinct. You can feel the energy coming from an object in your hand; people even appear more transparent as you begin to sense, see, smell, and even taste the energy coming from their auras. A walk in the park will be an entirely novel experience with your new way of sensing and gathering knowledge. It is exciting to see not only the physical form of a tree, for instance, but also its energy aura, which holds all the information about the tree from the time it was planted. You will be able to deduce its health, its age, and even its reaction to the weather—all from being able to tune in to its aura. This extra dimension of sensing is not just reserved for practicing psychics who work every day at developing their extra psi senses; everyone will be able to experience their extraordinary psychic capabilities.

During the Transition phase you will sometimes find yourself in a tug of war between the old way of sensing (logic and the physical senses) and the new (intuition and the psychic senses). You may still look for proof of auras, spirit guides, telepathy, or hauntings. Know that it's okay to look for confirmation if you need to. You are still a physical body getting used to your spiritual essence and energy-sensitive side. Eventually we will all become accustomed to living with our extrasensory senses, but it is the pioneers who will have the hardest time adjusting to the energy shift because they have to establish a new norm for the rest of us to follow.

During the Quickening stage you realized that some situations and relationships weren't good for you anymore. During the Transition phase many of these situations and people who aren't in alignment with your vibes will seem to drop out of your life. Fortunately, at this stage it is much easier to let go. Your life will completely change as you move into a world where matter doesn't matter as much as frequency and energy do. During this time it is also important for you to be open to recognizing your guides. These are basically your labor coaches who come to assist you in your transition to a more evolved be-ing. During this time you will also notice that things seem to line up in your life almost magically. Lightworkers, perti-nent information about the shift (such as what

It is normal to be paranormal.

is contained in this book), soul mates from other incarnations, and even messages from higher dimensional beings—any and all of these things will arrive exactly when they are needed. Something interesting happens when we begin to separate from our once-familiar ways: We begin to go with what feels right for us instead of focusing on what looks good to others. The Transition phase involves letting go of people, places, or things that keep us from attaining and maintaining our highest vibration.

In the previous chapter we talked about how your chakras are tied to your psychic senses. You are learning that *it is normal to be paranormal.* The very idea of extrasensory abilities still frightens the "old school" rationalists who prefer to leave everything to science. We can't deny science altogether (after all, it is the manifested child of the creative thinkers behind its theories), but traditional scientific methods may soon have to give way to alternative science that supports the idea of paranormal phenomena. As of now, however, the unfortunate fact is that most of us are more informed about our cell phones, computers, and televisions than we are about the features of our most important energetic possession, our extrasensory spirit. *Now* is the time for you to finally realize that you have extrasensory abilities that need to be expressed, fine-tuned, and properly maintained in order for you to expand your consciousness and ascend to the next level of awareness. The great thing is that once you become familiar with these amazing senses, you will be able to exert more control over the types of experiences you have; you will be able to exploit the full power of your true creative nature. This chapter will familiarize you with what you can expect to experience as you Transition, including some of the most common "symptoms" of this extraordinary phase.

Auras: Your Built-In Mood Ring

Most of us are familiar with the mood ring, a piece of jewelry that became a fad in the 1970s: The stone in the ring supposedly changes color based on the mood or emotional state of the wearer. As the stone reacts to body heat, observers can get an idea of whether the wearer is in a good mood or a bad mood based on the stone's color. Your aura is like a mood ring in that it changes color (and even size) according to its frequency and overall state. Everyone's aura has seven layers, or *subtle bodies*, that are nested within each other in a manner similar to a Russian nesting doll. There are three *physical plane bodies*, three *spiritual plane bodies*, and finally the *astral body*. The astral body provides the primary means of connection between the lower and higher bodies. The lower three bodies process energies dealing with the physical plane, while the upper three process energies from the spiritual planes. Each subtle body has its own unique frequency, but they are all inextricably linked and affect one another and the person's total energy charge.

> The astral body provides the primary means of connection between the lower and higher bodies.

During this phase you will begin to see and sense auras, which will allow you to gather information from dimensions beyond the physical world. Eventually first impressions will be almost entirely based on what you sense instead of what you see. For the sake of satisfying the rationalist in some of you, I will describe how auras appear through a certain type of photography known as Kirlian photography. This method has proven even to skeptics that there is an energy field or life force that emanates from and surrounds all living beings. In perhaps the best-known experiment, which involved cutting a leaf in half, the Kirlian images of the leaf still showed the leaf in its entirety, as though it had never been cut. The "memory" of the leaf's energy left an imprint in its aura, which showed up in the photograph. The resulting image provided a concrete demonstration of how energy is imprinted and held captive in an electrical field.

Likewise, when we see someone's aura, we are getting an impression of his or her emotional state, health, and overall state of mind based on the clarity, color, shape, size, and state of the aura. Holes or dents in the aura may signify energy leaks, illness, injury, or even an intrusion into someone's space in the form of violence. As you become more open and evolved, you will be able to see specific colors, whereas previously you may have only been aware of how someone else's energy felt. The fact is that every time you come in contact with someone, you exchange energy with that person. You may feel an instantaneous like or dislike depending on the quality of your auric interaction. You may notice that some people leave you feeling drained and depleted; such people may be living off your energy without your knowledge or consent. (I'll get more into these energy vampires in a later chapter.)

You can practice sensing auras by doing a very basic energy scan using your hands. Rub your hands together vigorously, pull them apart, and then slowly bring them back together again. As you do this you will feel resistance. This resistance is actually your aura. You have probably been sensing the auras of others without even realizing that you were doing it. You may have experienced their energy as an excited feeling, a tingly sensation, or possibly an intrusion if they were too far into your personal space. The feeling you get when someone of an unsavory nature is walking behind you is actually your own energy field detecting lower and possibly dangerous energy coming from that person. As you become better at sensing and reading energy, you'll be able to get a glimpse of each person's physical, emotional, mental, and psychic state almost as though you were watching a movie trailer. When you're really proficient you'll even be able to change your personal frequency to discourage and block nasty energy from coming near you.

Have you ever seen the heat waves on a highway or airport runway? Seeing auras pulsating with colors will now be as easy and natural as that. Every emotion has its own

> Seeing the auras of people, animals, and plants will now be a part of normal, everyday life.

color and frequency; they vary in hue depending on what is going on inside. Seeing the auras of not only people but also animals and plants will now be a part of normal, everyday life. When you look at someone now the first thing you do (usually unconsciously) is tune in to his or her vibes; eventually you will have the ability see these vibes as actual colors. Each color has a distinct frequency and resonates to a certain emotion and/or condition.

The **first (outer) layer** of the aura is the easiest one to see. Usually it ranges from milky white to cloudy gray, depending on the person's overall state. This layer aligns almost exactly with the shape of the physical body and acts as a protective shell against the outside world. You will be able to see it pull in and pulse out depending on whether or not the person is receptive or closed off. You may feel the energy coming from this layer in the form of resistance when someone doesn't want to be bothered, or a tingly feeling when someone is excited to see you. If you sense uneven energy coming from someone, it is most likely a sign that he or she suffers from energy leaks due to boundary issues, stress, or an irresponsible relationship with the darker, occult forces. He or she may also be an energy vampire who is trying to "refuel" on your energy.

This layer is linked to the Root chakra, which has to do with our connection to the physical world, our sense of safety, and our physical needs. As we evolve psychically we will be able to pick up the scent or smell of the first layer of the aura. Animals do this all the time. Wearing perfume and deodorant can mask the frequency of this outer layer, but as you become more attuned psychically you will be able to sense the true frequency underlying these artificial enhancements. Penetrating through to the inner layers of the aura may be difficult at first, because the first layer is quite dense.

The **second layer** of the aura holds emotions and feelings, including those from past (parallel) incarnations that are still exerting their influence. This layer can sometimes resemble a light show because the colors change and pulse according to emotions, feelings, and overall temperament. The colors are usually bright but can turn muddy if there is confusion or depression. Sparks of color can light up the aura like a fireworks display, especially during times of intense emotion. Maybe that is where the phrases "seeing sparks fly" (referring to anger) and "feeling fireworks" (during sex) originally came from. We can recognize where illness or disease may

Emotions are closely tied to our overall frequency.

manifest by looking at the second layer. This is because emotions are closely tied to our overall frequency; when our vibes go way down, we set ourselves up for potential health problems. The second chakra is closely tied to this layer of the aura because it corresponds to our creations and drama in the physical world, and is where our "taste" or zest for life originates.

Following is a list of the meanings of and correspondences for some of the colors that may be seen in a person's aura. As you read, keep in mind that layered colors will appear as tints when they are blended with white (thus indicating higher frequencies), and muddy when blended with black or darker colors (indicating lower frequencies). As you move through the Transition stage you will easily be able to interpret overlapping colors, vibrancies, and fragmented slices of color.

- ❋ **Red:** Life force, sex, survival instinct, passion, anger, frustration, blood/bleeding. Can indicate determination, a sense of importance, feeling overwhelmed, anxiety, or nervousness. A muddy red is usually deep anger.

- ❋ **Orange:** Sensuality, physical pleasure, emotional self-expression, creativity, impulsiveness, health, vitality. Can indicate an outgoing social nature or stress related to appetites and addictions. Dark orange may indicate an overly aggressive nature.

- ❋ **Yellow:** Mental alertness, analytical thought, happiness, optimism. Can indicate someone who is childlike or ego-driven. When yellow is murky and blended with a dark color or black, it can indicate resentment, jealousy, or a person who uses the power of his or her mind for negative purposes.

❊ **Green:** Healing, peace, nurturing, new growth. When the green is murky it indicates a person who is jealous, possessive, selfish, and manipulative. (This is where the phrase "green with envy" comes from.) A very murky green can indicate chronic depression, fear, or a need for security and balance.

❊ **Blue:** Verbal communication, free thinking, business, male energy, intuitive capabilities. Dark blue shades may indicate martyrdom or a victim consciousness.

❊ **Indigo:** Spirituality. Can indicate a person who has found or is seeking spiritual truth. This is the primary color found in the auras of Indigo children.

❊ **Royal blue:** Clairvoyance, spirituality, generosity. Can indicate someone on the right path or on the way toward new opportunities.

❊ **Lavender:** Imagination, vision, daydreaming, the ether. Can indicate a person who is in tune with other dimensions and realities. Murky lavender indicates someone who lives in his or her own world, who is poor at follow-through on commitments, and/or who does not handle money well.

❊ **Pink:** Love, tenderness, sensitivity, sensuality, artistic ability, affection, purity, compassion, self-love, tenderness, female energies, gay energies, emphasis on physical appearances. Can indicate a new or revived romantic relationship. Murky pink can indicate someone being nice at the expense of being truthful. Deep pink can indicate clairaudience (psychic hearing and channeling).

❊ **Purple:** Wisdom, authority, intuition, female energy, matriarchy. Can indicate a sense of superiority, a controlling nature, or a vivid imagination. Deep purple indicates possible incarnations as mystics or royalty.

❊ **Violet:** Selfless love and spirituality. Master teachers have violet auras. This color only appears when there is a commitment to spirituality or humanitarian causes.

- **Brown:** Practicality, earthiness. Can indicate a feeling of worthlessness, someone who is grounded or down to earth, an invalidating nature, or someone who emphasizes body over spirit. A murky gray-brown can indicate insecurity.
- **Black:** Death, hatred, lack of forgiveness, unresolved karma, malevolent intentions, shadow games. Usually indicates a long-term unforgiving attitude (toward others or self). If it appears in a specific area of the body it can signify health problems, unreleased grief, entities within a person's aura, or possession.
- **Gray:** Fear, health problems (especially if seen in specific areas). Greenish gray in certain areas indicates where an illness or disease has taken root.
- **White (cloudy):** Dogma, denial, organized religion, a lack of consciousness, cover-up, being good at the expense of being whole.
- **White (clear):** Spirituality, godliness, truth, Divine inspiration, compassion. Can indicate someone who sees the big picture, spiritually speaking. Often represents a new, not yet designated energy in the aura. White sparks indicate angelic qualities, new beginnings, or pregnancy.
- **Gold:** A high spiritual vibration representing integrity, respect, freedom, clarity, and awakened extrasensory senses. Indicates someone who has integrated spirit and body.

The more proficient you become at sensing and seeing the colors in the second layer of the aura, the more you will realize how transitioning into a world of higher frequency gives you enhanced insight when dealing with others in all aspects of life.

The **third layer** of the aura holds the mental body and has an even more subtle composition than the first two layers. This is where your thoughts and all your mental processes reside. This part of the aura is usually composed of a yellow light that radiates around the head and shoulders. The color will brighten if a person is deep in thought or concentrating. This is also where we hold our thought-forms, structured interdimensional energies that are the archetypes for our creations. Sometimes a thought-form will take on another color, particularly if there is a strong emotion connected with it. The mental layer of the aura connects to the Solar Plexus chakra and acts as a bridge between the higher and lower energy centers in the body. Because your thoughts will no longer be hidden from others who are evolved, you'll need to learn to protect this layer of your aura by placing a strong barrier of light around it and, if necessary, covering up its frequency at will. Conversely, you'll need to be extra cautious that your own clairvoyance doesn't turn into clair-*voyeurism*. Pirating someone else's ideas or thoughts is now as easy as tapping into an unsecured Internet connection.

> Sometimes a thoughtform will take on another color, particularly if there is a strong emotion connected with it.

The **fourth layer** of the aura, the astral layer, is the first one in the spiritual plane and connects directly to the Heart chakra. It has no clearly defined shape and is usually composed of clouds of color infused with a pinkish hue. It is through this layer that the physical body connects with the higher dimensions. It is the doorway to the astral plane. This layer will sometimes turn green during intense healings, as it is where all true healing occurs. With our evolved astral sight we will have the capacity to locate and examine any defects or diseases based on the appearance of this layer. We will also be able to tap into of all the emotions, passions, desires, and tendencies of others, even down to their very thoughts. Clearly we will all need to be cognizant of what we are thinking about—particularly when we're in public. At first, sensing and reading someone's aura will be easiest when we are in or near his or her energy field. As we evolve, however, we'll be able to do this merely by thinking of someone and connecting to his or her energy. This is similar to hacking into someone's Internet connection. (I will address proper astral ethics, protection, and privacy issues in a later chapter.) This layer of the aura is also tied closely to the emotions; when people fall in love it's not uncommon for them to have out-of-body experiences, especially during deep expressions of passion.

The **fifth layer**, the etheric template of the aura, corresponds to the Throat chakra and has a bluish hue. This is the blueprint that exists before the physical body is ever formed. It can only be seen by clairvoyants and master healers. This is another important layer in healing because it holds all the codes for the physical body. Just think: If we ever decipher this code, we could all have perfectly healthy bodies! As you may recall from the previous chapter, the psychic ability that corresponds to this chakra is the psychic sense of hearing. This is the layer where sound creates matter.

The **sixth layer**, the celestial light body, is the emotional level of the spiritual plane; it corresponds to bliss and spiritual ecstasy. It is where we reach interconnectedness with others and experience unconditional love. The colors of this body are soft pastels that glow and emanate softly from the body. This layer also corresponds to the Third Eye chakra in the center of the forehead. We use our psychic inner sight to perceive the world of spirit from this layer. It is from here that we receive and register emotional imprints from ourselves and others. This is where the physical mind connects to the spiritual mind through memories, dreams, spiritual awareness, intuition, and other forms of psychic knowing. The celestial light body holds our connection to something greater than ourselves: the universe.

The **seventh layer** of the aura, called the Ketheric or causal body, is the mental level of the spiritual plane. This body contains all the other bodies within it and often takes on the shape of an egg. This layer pulsates and vibrates at a very high frequency; here is where we *know* that we are one with the main source of the universe. This layer also contains the Kundalini force that runs up and down the body. When this force is awakened, our true spirit nature is finely tuned to a highly creative, magickal frequency. This layer of the aura relates to the Crown chakra and is what links us to the Divine. It contains the entire record of our spiritual journey, reflecting all of our soul's experiences through

> The celestial light body holds our connection to something greater than ourselves: the universe.

time. Before the advent of the empowering shift only highly developed lightworkers were able to access this layer of the aura. Clarity on this level means that one has the ability to experience one's true spirituality as part of daily life. This is also the most resilient level of the auric field.

Einstein and quantum physicists have explained that everything that exists is energy vibrating at different frequencies, and that physical matter, such as the human body, and energy, such as the aura, are really just two forms of the same thing. You will see that what is above actually materializes into what is below. Just as an embryo lives and grows inside the womb, experiencing a limited existence until it is ready to move on to the next phase of life in the outside world, we too are being pushed out into a world that gives us the opportunity to experience life at a higher frequency and dimension.

When the Past Is Still Present: Rebooting Your Karma

Karma is similar to a system of checks and balances that keeps track of everything you do. Heavy emotional imprints in the deeper layers of the aura can act as portals for unconscious patterns and behaviors to enter into and interfere with your psychic extrasensory nature. These karmic imprints need to be cleared out so you don't continue to repeat problems that are rooted in previous incarnations. Therefore, a big part of the Transition phase will involve clearing out any old consciousness programming, just as you would reboot your computer if it were constantly crashing. This is the painful part of Transitioning that I talked about at the beginning of the chapter. Once these old programs are identified, you can begin the process of resolving karma and getting on with your ascension to a higher vibration. Holistic healing modalities such as energy medicine, Reiki, and regression therapy will help you reboot your karma and realign your personal frequency with the evolving vibrations of the cosmos.

Karma is a system of checks and balances that keeps track of everything you do.

Before we do this, however, I first want to make sure that we all are using the same vocabulary. Let's start with the term *past lives*. A better term is actually *parallel lives*. Before the advent of the empowering energy shift, the idea of other lifetimes remained a mystery to many. It was easier to consider other lifetimes as part of a linear progression taking place in three-dimensional linear time. But the reality is that all lifetimes are occurring simultaneously in both space and time, making them *parallel* rather than *past*. We are streamlining into one frequency where the past, the future, and the present (our current state of consciousness, the Now moment) are now realized as one. This cosmic recipe of past, present, and future is now more correctly and accurately viewed as a concurrent string of experiences, different channels that we tune in to during our evolution into a higher, extrasensory state of awareness. Your parallel lives are still ongoing because they occur in space-time; they are still vibrating as a frequency, coded with information, out there in space. What you were used to conceptualizing as "past, present, and future" now flows as one frequency because in the higher dimensions, *there is no separateness*. As you move through the Transition phase you will gain a more precise understanding of how all of this fits into your expanded consciousness.

To recap what was covered in Chapter 2, during the Quickening phase of your evolution you learned about the impact of parallel lives, energy imprints, and our changing sense of time. During the Transition phase you will actually be able to will yourself into a particular incarnation and make corrections to that "program." This is how you release negative frequencies that are blocking your chakras and continuing to manifest in your life. You won't need to worry about running two consciousness programs or parallel lives at once because you will now have control over how and when you revisit an incarnation. Like the looking glass in *Alice in Wonderland*, the universe has become your magickal mirror. But there is no white rabbit with a watch telling you that it is late,

> In the higher dimensions, **there is no separateness.**

because time is an experience, not something to be ticked off in hours, minutes, and seconds. Episodes of déjà vu are really just a preview or precursor to the ability to time travel. Time travel occurs when you exit one universe or plane of existence and then reenter it at a different location. Once the full extrasensory psychic qualities of the sixth chakra kick in, you will be able to travel through wormholes and gateways to other realms at will in order to visit other incarnations. This is the way that more advanced life forms from other galaxies and star systems (which most dismiss as UFOs) dimensionally shift in and out of Earth's atmosphere. (More on that in the last chapter.)

> You will be able to travel through wormholes and gateways to other realms at will in order to visit other incarnations.

Clearing out parallel life issues and learned emotional responses and patterns during the Transition phase can be difficult and painful because emotions, the energy readouts from our chakra centers, are visceral (felt in the body). But we have the power to heal physical pain by going deep inside our own layers of consciousness, finding the energy blockages and misfires, and correcting our whole system. You can often ascertain which incarnations need clearing out by looking for hints on your physical body. Sometimes birthmarks and moles are clues to distant life trauma. Additionally, strong, deeply embedded emotions often manifest as physical conditions or diseases. Such embedded vibrations can throw off your whole emotional system, causing you to repeat destructive patterns of behavior over and over again. Once you begin to rid yourself of the heavy, dense vibrations you have accumulated throughout many lifetimes, you'll be able to run at a higher, more psychic frequency. To get a good understanding of what is encoded into your cosmic DNA, your deepest cellular memory from these past (parallel) lives, it is often worthwhile to get in touch with an experienced regressionist to help you connect the cosmic dots. A good regressionist can help guide you through other incarnations, realized relationships, lifestyles, traumas, and other pertinent life experiences so you can decide what you want to keep, what you want to jettison, and what you want to change. A regression (sometimes also called rebirthing) performed by a skilled professional can be helpful in filtering out parallel/past life emotions and traumas that are the cause of current problems, such as:

※ Phobias.

※ Health problems.

※ Feelings of guilt and anxiety.

※ Addictions.

※ Relationship issues.

※ Negative patterns.

Regression is a method of guided hypnosis that feels very much like watching a movie. You may pick up visuals from other lives, hear actual conversations, or just experience the accompanying sensations in your body during a regression session. Usually, the regressionist will begin the session with you lying down comfortably on a mat or couch and listening to some relaxing music. Once you're relaxed, the regressionist will begin a guided meditation, which will bring you into a state of hypnosis. You will have a chance to rewrite the script of what has gone unresolved from that particular lifetime. *You* have the power and ability to change the outcome because you are a creative being. Eventually you will be psychically skilled enough to go in and do it yourself simply by changing the vibration or frequency of your thoughts. As always, baby steps first.

Fortunately you do not need to examine every experienced lifetime because your spirit will intuitively know which ones to relive in order to make the necessary changes. You may also connect with guides who will maneuver you toward the areas that need to be corrected. In a sense, this process of evolution is bringing you back to your original factory settings—finely tuned, extrasensory, advanced, and much, much lighter.

Birthmarks, Moles, and Chronic Conditions

Sometimes we carry karmic debt and emotional memories much longer than we need to. As mentioned previously, the fifth layer of the aura is more or less a template for the lower physical body. This is the blueprint that exists before the physical body is formed. The sixth or emotional layer of the spirit may hold discordant energies, unwanted occupants, and discarnate and negative thought-forms that you have accumulated in your various incarnations. The energetic or spirit memory encoded in the aura body can sometimes manifest itself as a birthmark, mole, or chronic condition. These things provide a karmic trail of breadcrumbs that provides clues to our past lives. They can alert you to energy impressions from other incarnations that need to be released.

A port-wine birthmark is often thought to be a sign of having been badly burned in another incarnation, whereas other birthmarks may indicate a wound or trauma. I have a birthmark on my shoulder blade that marks where I was once stabbed in the back. A parallel/past life regression confirmed that I was attacked by a Viking warrior as I sat in the scriptorium of a monastery, copying ancient script by hand during the Dark Ages. This also helps explain why I hate it when anyone stands behind me while I am writing! Some Eastern cultures believe that moles can foretell one's fate. A mole on the face can mean a happy, cheerful disposition and a good life, whereas excessive moles on the face are often associated with seizures or epilepsy. A mole on the back can presage a life filled with burdens, whereas a mole situated on the chest signifies happiness, especially if it is near the Heart chakra. Moles on the feet indicate travel, and moles on the hand can indicate a talent carried over from a previous incarnation. You get the idea. Are moles and other marks really clues to our past karma or future fate? A very good book for further reading about birthmarks, moles, and birth defects is *Reincarnation and Biology: A Contribution to the Etiology of Birthmarks and Birth Defects* by Ian Stevenson. Stevenson was a biochemist, a professor of psychiatry, and head of the Division of Perceptual Studies at the University of Virginia, which investigates the paranormal. He did intensive case studies and wrote about children with birthmarks who showed uncanny proof of the type of death they suffered in a previous life. Some believe his studies provide conclusive proof of reincarnation.

Certain phobias and aversions are also associated with spirit memory. People who have been hanged or beheaded will often have chronic neck problems or hate the feel of anything tight around their neck. Some who have died in childbirth may find that they have difficulty conceiving children or have an aversion to having children. I myself have a fear of large birds, especially pigeons. During an in-depth aura assessment I found out why. I was beheaded during the 1500s for sorcery and my head was put on a post at the entrance gates to the city. Birds descended on my severed head and pecked at my flesh. To this day I don't like large birds because that energetic impression is so strongly encoded in my spirit memory. A lightworker told me that this particular life incarnation is the reason for my interest in high magick and mysticism, and that the clearing would have to be handled delicately so as to not interfere with what connects me to the Olde Ways (the work that I do as a healer, psychic, and astrologer). Realizing where my fear of large birds comes from actually diminished it to the point that it is now just more of a dislike.

Memory from trauma will stay in your aura throughout your every incarnation until it is healed and cleared. My Reiki teacher, Mary P. O'Donnell, had an amazing experience during a healing session to help find the source of her constant migraine headaches. Reiki is a form of healing that goes deep into the experiences, emotions, traumas, karma, and relationships of other incarnations that are trapped within the aura. Unlike regression, which brings you to a hypnotic state, Reiki is the process of moving blocked energy by using universal life energy channeled through the practitioner to the recipient. The group working on Mary all connected to the same frequency and, amazingly, linked to the traumatic memory associated with Mary's migraines. Mary began to recall what had happened to her when she was a monk in Tibet. She saw herself hanging on a pole and could feel rats gnawing at her feet. Amazingly, during the healing

Unexplained dislikes and phobias almost always originate in a different incarnation.

session everyone in the group simultaneously heard the sound of a Tibetan gong. They were able to shift dimensions *as a group* by linking to the same frequency. Mary has had other, similar experiences with her Reiki group, in which time was transcended and they had a collective experience of a parallel life in another dimension.

Unexplained dislikes and phobias almost always originate in a different incarnation. Previous life regressions are an excellent way to discover and resolve conflict and trauma, but you should always look to your body for physical clues first. It is liberating to recognize where we have come from because it clears the path to where we are going.

Rebalancing, Clearing, and Removing Blocks

During the Transition phase you have the opportunity to cleanse and balance your vital and subtle energies. Vibrations from emotional memory and cellular memory embedded in the aura may cause interference and static in your energy system, especially if the rogue frequencies are of a lower vibration that eventually manifest as disease or illness. Your emerging natural psychic abilities can malfunction and even be mistaken for psychosis or mental illness if there are too many unresolved, errant energies remaining in the subtle bodies and chakras. For example, during this time you may become extremely sensitive to energy and find it difficult to be around other people. If you are still attached to fears and traumas derived from other incarnations, you may have a constant feeling of impending doom or that something bad is about to happen. Clearly this can create anxiety. As mentioned previously, one of the most basic adjustments you can make during the Transition phase is to clear out any old consciousness programming. Undergoing a regression or Reiki session can help you identify deep-rooted problems within your aura, but it isn't always possible to run out and get a regression every time a negative vibration crops up. The good news is that you can learn to scan your own aura and fix the problem. As you Transition, fixing your own energy will soon be as easy as hitting the reset button on an electrical gadget.

A great deal of the negativity from parallel/past lives is connected to you via psychic connecting cords. These cords can keep you perpetually tied to a bad memory from a challenging relationship, a violent death, or some other negative, low vibration. In extreme cases possession can be the result, usually due to some very dark, parasitic energy within the aura. Once you identify what the problem is, through a regression, a personal scan, or even by following clues on your body, you can reset your vibration and remove the block. One way to do this is through physical acts such as smudging your environment with sage and letting the smoke waft through your aura, carrying any impurities away. Another method is to visualize these cords falling away and dissolving, which in turn transmutes or changes the negative energy into healing, positive energy.

Here is another example, this one drawn from personal experience. One day I just couldn't seem to get my act together. Everything was aggravating me, and I'm sure I was an aggravation to others. I attributed my mood to the fact that someone had angered me, and even though I knew better, I allowed my frequency to surge and short out my system. As I began to scan my own energy I kept getting locked into the same repeated thought, which of course only served to re-energize the current problem. I sent out a psychic S.O.S. to my friend JoAnn Ward, because if anyone could help me rebalance my energy, it would be her. Lo and behold my telephone rang, and when I looked at the caller ID there she was—my good friend JoAnn, an expert healer and lightworker. She had sensed that I needed an energy clearing and didn't seem surprised when I told her that I had just been thinking about her. She had simply connected to my thoughts and called me.

JoAnn instantly picked up on my energy and told me that I was running a parallel program, meaning that I was experiencing the same cord of contention with the same person but from a different life experience. I asked her to clear my aura and get rid of the negative coding that was interfering with my current consciousness. Like a psychic surgeon she skillfully began to cut and seal off the connecting cords that were still linking me to the cause of my irritation. She told me that I had had quite a few life experiences with the person who was currently triggering my frequency problem. She immediately saw that my adrenal glands were off, as well. This made total sense, because the adrenal glands are associated with the Root chakra, where we find grounding and our basic instinct for self-preservation. When this chakra is misaligned or blocked, feeling trapped by a problem in a kind of victim consciousness is often the result. Being a victim is paralyzing to the psyche because it can shut down your extrasensory senses, ramp up your emotions, and cause you to draw conclusions based on fear. JoAnn sent me different energy frequencies so I could reboot my emotional, physical, mental, and spiritual states. She tuned into my energy essence, reading where my chakras were out of balance, and began to clear out areas of my aura where the negative energy codes were lodged. She zeroed in on fears and problems from this life as well as other incarnated lives that were causing blockages. JoAnn healed the problem on a quantum level, which included all the incarnations I had had with the person who was aggravating me. As she worked on me I felt my energy change, and I felt sharper psychically, too.

Performing an aura diagnostic allowed JoAnn to rebalance my energy and transform the fear-based emotions that were causing the problem. I immediately felt very light, and I had a clear sense of knowing that my problem would not recur. Once my attachment to the negative emotional code in my aura was gone, JoAnn sent some white light energy to quickly fill the void and bring the space back to neutral. Once JoAnn sent the right frequency to the affected area, I could actually feel the negative energy lift off and out of my aura. The feeling—and the relief—was instantaneous. Amazingly, she did this clearing over the telephone. (She is a Reiki master who can perform long-distance healings.) After the clearing I figured out which unresolved issue was causing my etheric, emotional, mental, and spiritual upset. I recognized a pattern that kept repeating itself in my life—emotions that would ramp up every time I thought of or interacted with my nemesis. Thanks to the healing, I was able to extricate myself from the victim consciousness that had me believing that bad things "just happened" and instead embraced the manifestation mindset, which always believes that things happen *because of* you.

Scanning your own energy is a good daily habit to get into. Start by holding your hands palm side in on either side of your body, starting at your head. Gently feel your own aura and take note of any blockages or holes. A temperature differential, especially sudden coldness, can indicate a blockage or hole. Sometimes you will feel a depression or dimple in the aura, where it lies closer to the physical body. This can indicate a lack of energy or an imbalance. Psychic cords will have a thick, heavy feeling. Cords attaching you to a person or an embedded memory will siphon your energy and leave you feeling drained. They can also act as portals that let in negative energy. Because muscles hold emotional energy, it's common to have corresponding tightness or pain in the muscles associated with the blocked area. The neck and shoulders, in particular, tend to collect negative frequencies, which is why these spots are often tight with tension.

When you feel a blockage, stop and take a moment to find out what is keeping it there. Consciously ask the blockage to leave. If this is a chronic spot for tightness, delve into your memory bank and connect with the experience associated with the stress. It can be from a current situation or from a parallel/past experience that has lodged itself in your aura. It is usually something negative that is restricting the flow of energy and keeping you stuck. It simply needs releasing, and the frequency code needs to be reset. Start by cutting and sealing off all frequency cords associated with the blockage. Imagine seeing these cords pulled out, sealed, and destroyed right before your eyes. Maintain your focus while directing positive, white light energy into this area, remembering to relax and breathe deeply. I promise you that you will feel the energy move. Remember: You have the power to heal yourself! Continue with your energy scan until you reach your feet, making sure to run scans over your front and back so you can check all your organs and chakras.

Clearing out parallel/past life experiences doesn't mean that you lose the good, positive energy impressions from those experiences; only the fear-based imprinted emotions are transmuted to a more positive

Use your advancing psychic senses only for the highest good.

state. Fear-based emotions resonate with the frequencies of anger, disappointment, and other low vibrations. Fear itself is a terrible task master. Negative emotions are essentially "energy viruses" infecting your budding psychic abilities. The fact that the psychic dimensions exist in much higher frequencies means that you must be clear and balanced so that you use your advancing psychic senses only for the highest good. Psychic abilities misused for the purposes of manipulation can be a very dangerous thing for you because you may be unwittingly inviting contact with unknown negative entities.

Our new sensitivity to frequency will make us skilled at recognizing these kinds of imbalances. The same way that a "check engine" light goes on in a car to let you know that something is amiss, warning signals from our subtle body system will tell us if something needs attention. These warning signals are usually felt as an inner knowing—unless they go unchecked, in which case they manifest outwardly as an illness or other problem. When there is a blockage or imbalance in the chakra system you need to look for the faulty code held within the layers of the subtle body. It has to be changed, totally transmuted into a positive memory by focusing on the lesson instead of the teacher, in order to ensure that it won't keep interfering with your process of evolving and moving forward.

When you scan your own frequency, determine if there are any unhealthy attachments that you will need to let go of. If certain people just seem to know how to push your buttons and upset you, you have the power to tune them out and disconnect from their energy. Your upgraded psychic senses will make it easy to read their intentions by tuning in to your own energy to determine how it feels when you are around them. Do you feel good? Bad? Indifferent? Happy? Do you feel physically ill, with headaches or some other malaise? If you keep choosing the same type of negative relationships, if you have a chronic health condition, or if you seem to constantly have the same kinds of problems, you should perform a scan and/or meditate to see where the problem lies. Meditation brings you deep inside where the problem resides because it is rooted in you, not outside of you. All problems on the outside are just a reflection of and reaction to a code residing in your spirit body. Most likely they come from a fear-based emotion (usually from another incarnation) lodged in your aura. As you scan your energy, see yourself as a complete system that both inhabits and transcends the physical body, where you now have complete control over what stays and what goes.

Once you acknowledge where the problem lies, your fears will automatically begin to dissipate. You may work through them only to realize that there was never anything tangible there to begin with. Indeed, fear triggered by emotional memory is just an illusion. When you stop operating from fear consciousness you will open yourself to the higher psychic channels and begin to manifest positive situations in your life. Trust me when I say that deeply embedded negative memories will continue to show up unless you fix the root of the problem. Likewise, positive changes will engender more of the same, and your overall health (the physical body) will be maintained along with keener intuition and enhanced extrasensory abilities. Again, this is similar to the process of rebooting your computer and having it run at its fastest, most efficient speed.

> When you stop operating from fear consciousness you will open yourself to the higher psychic channels and begin to manifest positive situations in your life.

We are at a stage in our evolution at which we can consciously affect, for better or worse, each and every cell in our bodies by tuning in to a corresponding code or frequency generated by our own thoughts. Everything—thoughts, emotions, memories—has a vibration, and our job is to filter these vibrations and shield ourselves from what we don't want in our aura. Remember to ground your own energy every morning and night, and release yourself from any situations that have upset or drained you. Don't leave any unnecessary emotional cords tied to you because they will eventually deplete your energy. Cut those cords!

In addition, be aware of any repetitive negative verbal affirmations playing in your head. Repeated negative thoughts and patterns of behavior contribute to and often worsen those negative frequencies and blockages. Constantly thinking or saying such things as "I don't know where I am going to get the money," "I don't feel well," and "Things never work out for me" only serves to reinforce the negative imprint in your energy field. Many inherited diseases (*dis-eases*) are passed on through karmic cords. Releasing attachments to negative vibrations and disconnecting from harmful psychic cords allows you to be light enough to function in the higher extrasensory dimensions.

The completion of the Transition stage brings us to the Crowning state, the opening up of our true extrasensory nature. In the next chapter, we'll discuss our heightened awareness of the shift in consciousness as evidenced in synchronicities, repeated number patterns, and strange aches and "growing pains." All of this will be part and parcel of how you will become conversant in the new language of frequency.

CHAPTER 4

Crowning: Opening up to the New Language of Frequency

In childbirth, crowning occurs when the widest part of the baby's head (the crown) emerges from the birth canal and meets the outside world for the first time. Crowning is one of the most intense and painful phases of labor, but once it occurs the baby's arrival is usually imminent. Similarly, the Crowning phase of your evolution is an intense and exciting time, as your psychic senses begin to emerge in full. Although this involves more "labor pains," keep in mind that releasing old attachments and false beliefs will allow you to shift your frequency and experience existence in the higher

You are about to move out of the darkness and ignorance of third-dimensional consciousness and emerge into the higher realms of the cosmos and the Divine light of enlightenment.

dimensions. You are about to move out of the darkness and ignorance of third-dimensional consciousness and emerge into the higher realms of the cosmos and the Divine light of enlightenment. As we discussed in the previous chapter, the process of opening up to your highly evolved psychic nature requires you to keep a close watch on your frequency levels. This often involves clearing out lower vibrations that are causing imbalances or blockages.

Number Patterns

As you evolve, you may find yourself noticing number patterns more frequently. Do certain numbers seem to follow you around? Are they trying to alert you to something? Does something synchronistic happen every time you see a certain number? These numbers are actually a kind of binary code for our psychic awakening and evolution. The programs that support our full extrasensory awakening are pre-coded into our cellular memory, and numerical patterns are actually triggers meant to reset our frequency codes. They transmit symbolic messages that prompt us to accelerate our extrasensory evolution. One of the most familiar number patterns is 11:11 (as seen on a digital clock), and it is associated with the energy shift that links us to the higher dimensions. This numerical sequence is also linked to the universal concept of synchronicity; it is a prompt to look for the opportunities around us that will augment and hasten our evolution here on Earth. This pattern will activate our cosmic DNA and prepare us for our evolution to the higher dimensions. The 11:11 pattern is recognized all over the world. When you see it you are receiving a frequency upgrade that is more conducive to the ascension process into higher consciousness.

Certain number patterns resonate with different aspects of your consciousness and help you to remember what you already know—namely, that you come from the Divine creative source. In numerology the number 11 is considered a master number, meaning that it represents illumination and a channel into the Divine light, making it possible to have insight without rational thought. This number pattern resets the code for your Crown chakra and allows light to flow through you. The number 111 is a manifestation number, which indicates that what you think about you can also create. So keep your thoughts positive if and when you see this number. Repeatedly seeing 111 is always a precursor to some kind of manifestation, but if your intentions for creating are ego-based, the results will carry a difficult lesson with them. The pattern of 111 resets your creative code. As your thoughts take form you are reminded of the creative control you have, particularly as it pertains to your ability to manifest your hopes and dreams. The number 111 connects to your power center, which is also your passion center. You need to be mindful to create morally and ethically as well.

Other numerical patterns also seem to crop up frequently. Each number carries its own vibration and symbolic significance, and each marks a stage of your evolution as you move from one frequency to the next. These other numbers often take on a more personal synchronistic meaning and help remind you to connect more firmly to your life's purpose and personal evolution.

The number 2 awakens you to the fact that you are both a physical and a spiritual being, the duality within the one. The number *22*, like the number 11, is a master number that aids in manifestation. It also triggers a connection to your resilience and flexibility, and to the duality, polarity, and sensitivity found in the vibrational realm of twos. The number *222* resets your code to be in balance with the duality of the universe. The vibration of *222* initiates change and enables you to build on your knowledge step by step and gain confidence using your spiritual, psychic senses.

The number 3 is a sacred number in many belief systems and religions. Freemasons, for example, revere the 33rd degree of their order. In magickal rituals many actions are performed three times. This number is also is the linking code for streaming the past, present, and future into one experience. Under *Sharia* (Muslim law) a man can divorce his wife by repeating the phrase "I divorce you" three times. There is scientific evidence that the brain takes three days to register complete shutdown, even when all other bodily systems are failing. This is because the astral or emotional body stays connected to the physical body for three days after death. The number 3 is interesting in that it codes you to several different frequencies depending on how many 3s you see at one time. A single 3 stimulates the magick of manifestation that we all possess. It represents the unified workings of the body, mind, and spirit. It also acts as a bridge between the higher and lower energy chakra centers on the body and the corresponding areas within the aura. This number also activates your intuition.

The number 4 is tied to the four quadrants of the earthly plane (north, south, east, and west), the four elements (earth, fire, air, and water), and the four phases of the moon. When you see the number 4 show up alone or in sequence, it signals change and ending. There are some people who don't like the number 4 in an address because it often portends a move, a divorce, or some other concluding event. Seeing the number 444 will reset your inner code to accept the persistence of the spirit even after the body and material world have passed away. Fortunately this number frequently presages an ending that ultimately leads to a new beginning.

The number 555 indicates progression and positive change. Those of us who tend to get stuck in a rut will often notice this number pattern crop up. If this happens to you, it will help you reestablish your connection into the universe and resonate with the frequency necessary for making changes and getting on with your life.

The number 666, the so-called mark of the beast, resets your code for how you view the material world and the physical body. It is actually a reminder not to live only in the material world of illusion, where attachment to things often takes precedence over the soul and spirit. The number 666 is about illusion and false beliefs that rob the spirit of its ability to ascend. The illusory world of materiality is similar to a sticky web that that entraps us. Could the "number of the beast" represent money, big banks, Wall Street, religious dogma, or any type of organization or paradigm in which disinformation and fear are used for control? When you notice this number, remind yourself that there is more to the world than just material possessions. It shifts you into being more conscious of how the "beast" (read: false beliefs) attempts to keep you from evolving beyond the third dimension of physical form. This number also codes to the collective memory of being created by an alien race of more advanced beings and genetically manipulated for the purposes of enslavement.

The number 7, whether seen alone, in triplicate, or combined with other numbers, will reset your frequency to bring about transformation through agency and motion. This is actually one of the most powerful numbers for triggering a subconscious response. Hippocrates himself said that it "keeps together all existing things with a secret power and it also has an effect on planets." There are seven notes in the diatonic scale in music. This number codes to your ability to self-heal. Simply by using your voice, tapping, or playing a musical instrument you can actively enter into the state and process of healing. When you see the number 777 it helps restore your system back to perfection by deleting all unhealthy, negative thought codes or frequencies from your subtle body. When you are feeling overwhelmed or out of sorts, visualize the number in your head—or better yet, say the words *seven, seven, seven* out loud to induce self-healing.

The number 8 is the number of the cosmos itself and resets your code to infinity. The Arabic number even resembles the symbol for infinity, with the center point representing the present moment, the Now. When you see several 8s in a row you sync up with the moment and are given keen awareness of what you have created in your life. The moment is an infinite blip of awareness, that point of intersection between where you have been and where you are going. You will often see the number 8 as you transition into higher consciousness. This number also often accompanies the awakening of Kundalini energy, the primordial cosmic energy in every individual that is coiled like a serpent at the base of the Root chakra.

The number 9 has some very interesting properties. It is the only number that, multiplied by any number, always reproduces itself—for example, 9 times 2 equals 18, and 8 plus 1 equals 9, and so on with every number it is multiplied by. This number helps us remember that, no matter what we experience or how many times we incarnate, we will always remain the same eternal spirit energy. When you see the number 9 you recode and sync up with the completion of a cycle. It represents a clearing of old energy, allowing for new energy to flow in as you reach the next phase of your evolution. Seeing the number 999 helps activate the hidden codes in your DNA and moves you into a higher frequency. It signals the completion of your life in the physical world and opens the connection to your higher self. The number 9 is usually accompanied by a synchronistic event that supports or proves the existence of other dimensions—for example, receiving a message from someone who has passed over. These messages are usually cryptic, however, so look for the meaning in random songs you hear, on road signs, in the people you meet, or via some other means of communication. A *novena* (a recitation of prayers and devotions for a special purpose, recited for nine consecutive days) is known to fulfill specific requests and even bring about miracles. Any iteration of this number advances us spiritually and reveals the next phase of cosmic energy that will be made available to us in the higher dimensions.

Synchronicity

All numbers have a duality, just as the universe itself does. Numbers activate the left side of the brain through logical problem-solving, and also the right side of the brain, which uses the vibrations from numbers to tap into intuition. Even though I was terrible at math because of all the left-brain logic involved, the mystical language of numbers always resonated with my esoteric side. Most of us have a lucky number or sequence of numbers. I once had a client who always heard from a particular guy she was interested in every time she saw a certain number. Could that be the secret number code that synced up with the frequencies of these two people here and also in other life incarnations? Another client of mine would always see the number pattern 996 every time she was about to have a car problem. You have to wonder who or what on the other side of the cosmic veil was doing this! Perhaps the three-digit number was a kind of cosmic area code that enabled her to connect to spirit help from the higher dimensions. I too have noticed that certain numbers or series of numbers have cropped up in the various phone numbers I have had throughout the years; these same numbers have also corresponded to specific dates that are personally meaningful.

Numerical patterns are also at play in the unseen frequency waves of our thoughts. All frequencies can be reduced to numbers because they have wavelengths that can be counted and measured. When our own frequency hones in on or resonates with the frequency of someone or something else, this brings about a synchronous event or events "by chance." These events can be either positive or negative, but they usually have a distinct purpose. When you bump into someone you haven't seen for years and you were *just* thinking about that person, and when that person confirms that he or she was just thinking of *you*, you have synchronicity. What has happened here is that your thoughts intersected somehow, and the thought energy materialized into reality, which is what caused you to meet. Your combined thoughts synced up and, in a kind of spiritual alchemy, found expression in the physical world. Shifting into a higher frequency will open the door to synchronistic events in your life. The neat thing about synchronicity is that the more aware you are of these events, the more often they will occur. The operative word here is *aware*. When you function in a state of higher awareness, your thought creations will become more and more apparent. This is nothing to be distressed about; rather, it is a wonderful outcome of the new language of energy that should be embraced. It will be easier to recognize synchronicity if you reflect back on how certain events and circumstances in your life just seemed to line up and fall into place, seemingly by magick. Synchronicity is just one way the universe communicates with us by syncing our thoughts up with the master creative force of the cosmos. The more you evolve and grow into your higher extrasensory capabilities, the easier it becomes to sync up with and manifest your needs and desires.

Synchronicity also teaches us that there is more than one way for things to come about. You limit your choices by limiting your thinking and not being open to all possibilities. Staying positive is important in this respect; even the slightest hint of doubt or negativity can bring about undesired results. The only consolation for such an unpleasant event is the lesson you (hopefully) learn, which in turn will help you evolve. The synchronicities and coincidences of everyday life bring the exact people, things, events, and/or circumstances needed into your life to further your evolution. Synchronicity reminds us that the universe and everything and everyone in it are connected on an energetic level. Whether consciously or unconsciously, everything and everyone is working together to bring you the support and guidance you need as you evolve along with the cosmos.

What about miracles? Aren't they a form of synchronicity too? Miracles are, by definition, amazing events brought about through Divine intervention right when they are needed the most. Miracles are your strongest intentions coming from the center of your spiritual creativity. They cut through all the cosmic chatter and link directly into the Divine creative force itself. It is like bypassing your immediate supervisor and going straight to the boss for help. Miracles show us that even the most hopeless situations can be turned around. Synchronistic events can be romantic, exciting, subversive, disconcerting, disturbing, and even miraculous, but they all reflect how tied in we are to the creative force of the universe as we transition to the higher dimensions during our spiritual evolution.

> Miracles are your strongest intentions coming from the center of your spiritual creativity.

(Re)Birth Pains

Your evolution won't come without a few signs and symptoms to alert you that the process is underway. You can be sure that none of these symptoms were covered in high school health class or biology 101, because we never had a vocabulary for them—until now. Learning about these symptoms will also help open the doors to energy medicine, a new, improved form of healthcare. The important thing to remember is that this is not a one-size-fits-all proposition. Because we all code to our own specific frequency, the evolutionary process will be different for everyone; a lot will depend on how open each person is and how much negativity he or she is carrying. With this in mind, following are some common symptoms—rebirth pains, I call them—of this phase of the evolution.

You can expect to experience some **emotional pain** as you clear out deeply embedded negative vibrations. Revisiting painful situations is the first step in healing them because it allows you to come to terms with the origins of the memories. Suppression and/or denial is never a solution. You can't treat the emotional pain of memories successfully unless you release the deep-rooted vibrations held in the energetic body as stored negative frequencies. As you begin the process of releasing the negative frequencies associated with these emotions, the pain will likely be heightened by the fear of the unknown, particularly as you feel yourself changing. This begins the process of emotional clearing, letting go and clearing out the old, stuck, low-frequency emotions such as anger, grief, sadness, and bitterness that come along with embedded memories and wounds. Think of it this way: Even people who undergo extreme plastic surgery in order to improve their appearance have to adjust on an emotional level

The loss of familiar behavior paradigms is bound to create emotional instability and even grief.

to their changed body as well as to the reactions of others. Emotional turmoil and blockages will take many forms—depression, anxiety attacks, food cravings, and moodiness, just to name a few. These emotional upheavals are also due to the fact that you are becoming more empathic. Empaths have the ability to feel and to sometimes even take on the pain of others because they are so sensitive. As you evolve psychically and become more connected to the frequency of the collective consciousness, you will be able to read, connect with, and hopefully heal the pain of others.

Finally, you may realize that there are just some things and people that you have to let go of because their vibration is no longer in sync with your higher state of being. The loss of familiar behavior paradigms is bound to create emotional instability and even grief. I have had some clients tell me during their psychic counseling sessions that things just don't seem real to them anymore. They feel as though everything they once believed in, from relationships to religious beliefs, has let them down. What is happening is that their emerging psychic senses are widening the scope of their perceptions. They can now feel, taste, smell, and see the energy around them. They know that the physical is not all there is, and this can be an upsetting realization at first.

And then there are the **psychic-logical problems** that may occur, as your way of sensing and gathering information about the world shifts radically. As you evolve, your physical senses may take a back seat, while feeling, intuiting, and sensing will assume a more primary role. You may even feel a bit crazy at times as your psychic senses start to assert themselves in earnest. Know that you are not alone in this. Even old-school materialists will experience the shift in energy and the accompanying sensations and symptoms on some level. Unfortunately, those who fight the change will not be able to sustain themselves for very long in the higher frequencies. The influx of accelerated vibrations will shatter false beliefs the way a high-pitched note shatters glass.

Physical Symptoms

Nothing in this book is intended to take the place of medical advice from a medical professional. But please also consult with a holistic healer who will help you find the energy imbalance in your subtle body that may be aggravating or even causing the physical condition(s).

Traumas are stored as energy blockages in the layers of your aura and as cellular memories in the physical body. Certain negative emotions are stored in particular organs in the body. Anger, for example, is stored in the liver. Bitterness and regret are stored in the pancreas; fear is stored in the kidneys; and grief, hatred, and disappointment are stored in the heart. As we clear each of these blockages from the emotional body, the physical body will release its equivalent cellular memory. It's common to feel physical discomfort during this process. Healing must be done on *all* levels. Holding on to painful emotional memories will often manifest as a physical condition or disease (*dis-ease*), so it's imperative that we go through this often-painful process in order to ascend. Some of the physical discomfort you will feel will also be the result of your body changing to accommodate your expanding chakra system. This will include an integrated brain that will merge the capabilities of both the left and right hemispheres. You may also experience cravings for certain foods along with stomach upset, because you will need to adapt your diet to your lighter, spiritual body.

Let's start with **ascension headaches**. This type of headache is very distinct from any other kind (for example, a tension headache or a migraine) in that it always seems to be limited to the top of the head where the Crown chakra resides. You may feel pressure, as if your head were about to explode, along with an itchy or tingly feeling over your entire head. This is caused by the opening of the Crown chakra as we download programs from the new frequency. The tingly or itchy feelings come from a buildup of static electricity. The best way to cope with an ascension headache is to go with the flow of the energy and know that it will pass after your own vibration adjusts to the energy you just absorbed. Yawning sometimes helps to relieve the pressure. At some point in the future we may have a choice of headache pills: migraine, tension, sinus, and ascension.

Speaking of which, **sinus problems** are also common, even if you've never had a sinus problem in your life. We all know that mucus in this area acts as a barrier against outside debris and irritants; on an energetic level, excess mucus can also indicate that you are clearing out old belief patterns and getting rid of irritating/distressing people or situations in your life. Massaging both sides of your nose close to your eyes and pressing your index fingers under your nostrils above your lip should activate the acupressure points to alleviate any pain you are experiencing.

As we become more accustomed to using our third eye or psychic vision, our eyes will take on a temporary backseat role.

Many people will experience **vision problems,** even if they are wearing the proper corrective lenses. As we become more accustomed to using our third eye or psychic vision, our eyes will take on a temporary backseat role. This is analogous to wearing a patch over your good eye in order to exercise a lazy eye and encourage it to work better. Many people have told me that they have required stronger and stronger prescriptions due to the rapid changes in their eyesight. In addition to vision problems, you may also experience eye tics and twitches. Like a flashing light on a piece of electronic equipment that alerts you that something is wrong, these tics are alerting you to reset your energy. Once you become accustomed to the new frequency and attuned to your psychic vision, the twitching should stop. You also may find yourself blinking a great deal for no apparent reason. During your evolution a great deal of past trauma from other incarnations will be released, and blinking is part and parcel of the natural process of clearing encoded memory from your physical and spiritual systems. Indeed, in Rapid Eye Technology (RET), a new form of energy medicine, several techniques are used to release trauma, including blinking. Practitioners of RET are well aware of how eye movements and blinking can affect emotions. Purposeful blinking can be used to release stress as well as any negative energy residing in your physical and spiritual bodies.

Have you suddenly experienced a buzzing or ringing in one or both of your ears? This freaky frequency may be a form of **temporary transitional tinnitus** (not to be confused with the medical condition). Sometimes normal sounds will suddenly seem louder because your physical sense of hearing is going through similar changes. You may suddenly hear a mix of white noise, beeps, tones, buzzing, whooshing, static, roaring, or ringing in your ears. There is also something called *audio dyslexia*, a condition in which sounds of letters and words are jumbled or distorted, which makes comprehension difficult. Hearing any voices in your head lately? Most likely you are not schizophrenic—just an up-graded member of your species able to tune in to the higher frequencies of other dimensions. Admittedly, when you first tune in to a conversation from a parallel life and hear the whole thing as if you were there, it can be a really strange and disorienting experience. But you *are* there, in a sense, because your energy field is still connected to that experience.

Your evolution can also cause **adverse reactions to food.** Foods and ingredients you once reached for on the supermarket shelves may now revolt you. It is very common to look at something as prosaic and common as a bag of potato chips and suddenly get an awful taste in your mouth. This happens because you have become sensitive to the energy frequencies coming from the preservatives in the chips. If it isn't good for you, you will actually taste the lower vibration! You can find out what foods work with, instead of against, your new frequency by placing what you are thinking of eating up against your stomach. You will either feel confirmation to go ahead and eat it, or you will feel physical discomfort, which means you should probably put it down and find something else.

Not a few bodyworkers have told me how their clients seem to have considerably more **muscle aches and pains** these days, especially in their necks, shoulders, and backs. This is due to all those cellular memories from emotional pain that need to be cleared. Massage, Reiki, and acupressure can work wonders. The shoulder blades, sometimes called the angel wing area, may get especially sore due to your newly enhanced and attuned Heart and Thymus chakras. One way to relieve this problem—some say the *best* way—is to pull gently on your ear lobes; this often helps to release tension throughout the entire muscle group.

As I mentioned in the previous chapter, the expanding Heart chakra can cause **tachycardia** (rapid heartbeat). This condition is different from medical tachycardia related to traditional cardiovascular problems, because it is brought on by our evolution. Sudden jumps in heart rate, the kind of feeling you

The wavelike structure of the heartbeat resembles the wave structure of the entire universe.

experience when you are anxious or excited, are basically just a symptom of the Heart chakra opening and enlarging to receive more energy. If this happens to you, ask yourself what emotional memories you need to heal. What relationships, current or past, require healing and closure? As an aside, it is very interesting to note that the wavelike structure of the heartbeat—the sine wave—resembles the wave structure of the entire universe. This could be one of the reasons why the heart plays such a vital role in our evolution.

Going through the Crowning phase can sometimes produce **flulike symptoms** such as congestion (a result of the detoxification process), a sore throat (due to the higher vibrations of speaking with intent), and sore muscles and feet (from the energy of moving forward). These flulike symptoms can also be caused by the high-level frequencies emanating from solar storms. The energy of solar storms actually contains the new coded frequency information that activates your "junk" DNA and your extrasensory senses. Studies indicate that ESP accuracy heightens during rapid geomagnetic pulsations, which should be no surprise, because these pulsations are due to turbulence and disturbances in the natural magnetic field surrounding the Earth—which are in turn caused by interaction with plasma, the electrically charged gas given off by the sun during solar storms.

Changes and fluctuations in weight during the Crowning phase seem to bother people the most. The extra weight acts as a grounding mechanism for the new, higher frequency that you are pulling into your system. Fat also acts as an insulator for the nervous system: Because your psychic evolution makes you more electrically charged than ever, you may need the extra insulation until you adjust to the higher vibrations. Some of this weight gain will be the result of excess water weight; this occurs because water is a natural conductor of electricity. Don't run out and load up on salty foods in the hopes that you will draw in more psychic electricity, because you will only wind up throwing your whole body off balance. Let your body find its balance and decide how much water it wants to hold onto. The most important thing is to drink plenty of purified water to keep your system clean and clear. Conversely, weight loss is also possible, especially if you are clearing out a lot of heavy emotional burdens. Eventually your weight will level off and redistribute to accommodate your changing physical form. Such changes will a include a larger diaphragm that is better adapted to more purposeful breathing, as well as a slightly elongated head to accommodate the changing brain.

Your evolution will see the development of four new organs.

One of the more noticeable (and thankfully temporary) physical changes is the **Buddha belly**. This is altogether different from a beer belly or the love handles that seem to come with age. The Buddha belly comes about because both the lungs and diaphragm are growing so you can breathe more deeply, mindfully, and purposefully. The development of the diaphragm is important to the complete ascension process. In addition to a larger diaphragm, your evolution will also see the development of **four new organs**. Two of these organs will be responsible for removing any decay that is blocking the awakening of your psychic senses. They will act as filters for the body's new crystalline structure. These two organs will reside slightly above the hipbones, which will also increase the size of the lower abdomen area. The other two new organs will lie under the ribcage just above the kidneys. They will produce a new kind of cell that will collect and distribute photon (light) energy to every cell in the body. If you don't have a Buddha belly or any of these other physical signs and symptoms, don't worry. It doesn't mean that you will be left behind as everyone else ascends. Just as every pregnancy is different, so is each person's evolutionary trajectory. Much of this has to do with what has already been encoded in your DNA as well as your karma. Incidentally, many of the "symptoms" of ascension will mimic the hormonally driven symptoms of pregnancy and/or menopause, even in men.

Have you been waking up in the middle of the night lately? **Interrupted sleep** can also be a part of this stage of your evolution. It is not unusual to be jolted awake at exactly the same time, night after night. (As I discussed in the previous chapter, these are prompts or coded number patterns that are resetting your system to clear out old emotional programs.) People seem to awaken most frequently at 3:18 a.m. and 4:44 a.m. The number 318 codes us to the magick of manifesting in the moment; the number 444 lets us know that the physical body and material world are changing to accommodate our existence at a higher frequency. In this way you are upgraded during the night in the same way that a program on a computer is upgraded.

Getting proper sleep is extremely important because your body produces melatonin during the night. This is an important neurotransmitter that affects your circadian rhythm or biological clock, which is also changing to resonate with the frequencies of higher consciousness. Resetting your internal clock helps your body upgrade and repair the vital organs that are now taking on a higher vibration and becoming more attuned to the energy shift. Your physical body works along with your subtle body to process the higher frequencies that are awakening your extrasensory abilities.

The precise time you are awakened can also clue you in to what emotion or emotions need to be resolved. Many people notice that they frequently wake up between 1 a.m. and 3 a.m. without the help of an alarm clock. This is the time for the liver to replenish itself, so if you keep waking up between these hours there's a good chance you need to clear out some anger in order to continue progressing in your evolution. The corresponding energy center you will want to look at is the Solar Plexus chakra. Gall bladder issues will wake you up between 11 p.m. and 1 a.m. This organ is usually associated with feelings of intense anger and rage. Psychological pressure, stress, irritation, annoyance, and frustration weaken the flow of the energy in the gallbladder. If you find that you keep waking up during these hours, there is likely an imbalance in this chakra. This chakra is the center of your personal power, the place of ego, passions, impulses, strengths, and,

Your physical body works along with your subtle body to process the higher frequencies that are awakening your extrasensory abilities.

yes, anger. Anger issues will block you from experiencing and effectively using your extrasensory gifts.

Unless you are naturally an early riser, an imbalance in the large intestine will wake you up at the crack of dawn, sometime between 5 a.m. and 7 a.m. The large intestine is where you hold your guilt, grief, and regrets. If you have issues with holding on to the past and/or a fear of letting go during the evolutionary shift, your second (Sacral) chakra is most likely out of balance. If you feel blocked creatively and your sex life is less than what it ought to be, you'll need to work on clearing out issues related to this energy center, which is associated with clairgustation, or psychic taste. This is all about the basic "energetic taste" of your life experiences. Ask yourself, *Is my life sweet or bitter to the taste?* It's important to let go of all fears and insecurities to fully appreciate all the good in your life.

Insomnia is also possible, but before you reach for a sleep aid, stop and realize that you are probably just having a power surge due to the amount and quality of energy that you are taking in during your waking hours. When you are psychically open, any exposure to outside energy will have an effect on your own energy, either by overstimulating you or draining you. In time you will know when and how to close off your energy centers to outside frequencies.

> Let go of all fears and insecurities to fully appreciate all the good in your life.

As you shift into becoming more psychically attuned it is very common to have **bizarre, intense dreams.** With these dreams you are merely releasing old energy as you connect with your other incarnations to access knowledge you need in your current life. I once had a medical condition for which I was seeking treatment. One night I had a very lucid dream that connected me to my incarnation as a Chinese holistic doctor in the 16th century. I woke up from the dream knowing exactly what vitamins and treatment I needed to remedy the condition. In the days following the dream, I synchronistically happened upon precisely the books and information I needed. I have since learned to program myself to ask for needed information about tough situations before going to bed. I always seem to find what I need that way.

A sudden change in job or career is another common "side effect" of the evolutionary process. The need to be authentic and true to yourself is part and parcel of going through the energy shift, and so a job with limited potential or stultifying conditions often just won't cut it anymore. Finding your passion usually isn't about the money, but if you are doing something you love, the cash is sure to follow. As you open yourself to your psychic energy and manifesting abilities, it is important to move away from situations that engender negative thought-forms. Rather than continuing to dwell on how much you hate your job, use your creative abilities to bring about the perfect situation.

You may find yourself **withdrawing from relationships.** Perhaps you can no longer stand your spouse, partner, or significant other, even though you have been together for a very long time. Boredom can set in in any relationship, but I am talking about leaving someone on practically a moment's notice. You wake up one day and realize that your frequencies no longer dovetail, and—*adios*. Once all the old karma has been resolved you are able to release the bonds of the old relationship and cut any binding cords. Some relationships change but are not completely severed. A lot depends on how you connect energetically to the other person: Are you on the same wavelength? It is very normal to not want to be in relationships that impose limits on you during this phase. The need to feel free is a driving force behind many separations, falling-outs, and divorces. Issues stemming from fear, distrust, jealousy, and possessiveness are antithetical to the new frequency. Your enhanced psychic abilities will enable you to see through shams and lies.

You will likely have days when you just can't seem to get it together, when time seems to fly by and you can't catch up. This is the **"fast time"** that comes about when linear time and space merge and morph into space-time. Hours, days, and months seem to stream right by you, making you wonder where all the time went. It may be difficult to concentrate and hold a thought for more than a few moments; I call this ADD: **ascension deficit disorder.** You may also find yourself searching for words and sometimes even saying things backward. Rest assured that this is normal as your brain adjusts to the higher frequencies running through your body. Finally, simple tasks may seem to take forever, and more complex ones can be as challenging as climbing Mount Everest. Again, all normal for this phase.

As if all this weren't enough, you may also experience **strange food cravings.** The physical body is looking for a way to ground some of this intense energy flowing in through the subtle body. For this reason you may find yourself craving foods rich in vitamin B, which supports the nervous system, helps reduce stress, and gives your body energy. My friend JoAnn once craved oatmeal, a rich source of vitamin B, during this phase of her ascension. The oatmeal had a very grounding effect on her and provided what her body needed during the energy shift. Your evolution requires specific nutrients during each stage of development, and your body will *always* crave what it needs. The vibrations of foods will either be appetizing or a complete turn-off. Many people become really turned off to the idea of eating meat and look for other foods to supply them with protein. The vibrations from slaughtered animals resonate with fear, and those highly sensitive psychic centers opening up can often pick up on that. Personally I love animals so I don't even want to go there or think about it.

Your evolution requires specific nutrients during each stage of development.

You may want to indulge in some fattening food from time to time because your internal wiring needs the extra insulation. Craving food that is high in fat is natural during the shift, so don't deny yourself, but only eat until you are full. Don't gorge yourself to the point of feeling overstuffed or sick. Because of the ways in which your body's cells are changing you may also find that you suddenly have strong cravings for sugar and salt. Salt craving can also come from night sweats and hot flashes that occur as your body burns off the denser energies. Evolving really is a lot like menopause. Sorry, men!

Miscellaneous Signs

Getting used to your newly activated psychic channels may take some time, especially for those who aren't familiar with the nature of

Getting used to your newly activated psychic channels may take some time.

higher dimensional capabilities. Fortunately, teachers and guides will come into your life to assist you during the Crowning phase. As the saying goes, "When the student is ready, the teacher arrives." Teachers don't always have to be people; they can come to you in the form of circumstances or even through the books you read (perhaps this one!). Anything that offers you the opportunity to recognize and use your psychic senses will be part of the lesson plan. Because you are no longer bound by logic alone, the mind has to make way for the expression of the spirit. The spirit pushes you to rise above the third dimension and gives you the capabilities to feel, sense, and create whatever you wish. This is where the good stuff comes in.

Let's start out with the initial awakenings of your emerging psychic side. You may find yourself suddenly inspired to change or create something, or you might come up with a brilliant idea, even if you don't have a creative bone in your body. **Flashes of inspiration and bursts of creative energy** may at first make you feel as though your spirit were on crack, because grandiose ideas seem to be flowing in from all directions. Staying grounded is more important now than ever as you download the creative "apps" that will help you make your ideas a manifested reality. You may also suddenly have talents that you never knew you had, such as playing a musical instrument, writing, drawing, or singing that goes far beyond your karaoke in the local bar or your solo performances in the shower. Many of these talents were active in other incarnations and thus were encoded in your subtle body system. Now they are being made available to you once again.

Your new, extrasensory frequency will interact with electrical gadgets such as computers and household appliances, causing them to malfunction and even break at times. Keep an extra supply of light bulbs and batteries around, and invest in extended warranties, because as you tune in psychically, some of your electrical possessions are sure to tune out. In similar fashion, I have learned from experience to keep overly agitated, hyper, all-over-the-place types of people away from my possessions, including my car. I have had ungrounded people actually cause my electrical gadgets to break. I myself have short-circuited more than a few coffee pots, vacuum cleaners, and hair dryers.

Shape-shifting will be the new plastic surgery. As you evolve and delete heavy, dense, encoded vibrations, your physical body will take on a more vibrant and youthful appearance. You know how terrible you can look when you don't feel well or when you are in a relationship or job that lowers your vibration; you are responding to the surrounding energy in both appearance and attitude. "Shape-shifting" doesn't mean that you will look like an entirely different person: Rather, you will look like a younger, better version of yourself due to the more precise alignment with your subtle body. The empowering shift will also give you access to the youth and vitality gene deeply encoded within your DNA.

> Shape-shifting will be the new plastic surgery.

You may also experience **heightened sensitivity to your surroundings.** Crowds may suddenly bother you because every time you walk past someone, you will sense his or her energy. That's a lot of information to take in! Until you learn to keep energy boundaries, being around large groups of people can make you feel extremely anxious and disoriented. Another thing to be prepared for is possible **encounters with interdimensional beings.** (You may be more familiar with the term *alien*, which is just another name for the same thing.) As you will learn in a later chapter, these beings have influenced the beginning of human civilization itself. They operate on a level that we call "paranormal" because their high frequency enables them to travel through time, communicate via telepathy, and exhibit advanced extrasensory powers. When it comes to actually communicating with interdimensional beings and spirit entities you will need to be very discerning and learn to recognize which ones are dark and which ones are light. Being psychically open can leave

> Another thing to be prepared for is possible encounters with interdimensional beings.

you vulnerable to spirit possession from a wayward entity that, for whatever reason, wants to toy with your emerging psychic senses. Having extrasensory awareness and powers doesn't mean that it is safe to let your guard down. Some spirit entities are tricksters and even demonic in nature. You have to be careful out there in your new energetic habitat.

Finally, you will definitely experience **increased psychic and intuitive abilities**, including clairvoyance, out-of-body trips, telepathy, and other psychic phenomena. Once you start being able to read someone's thoughts and know what someone is going to say before he or she say it, you will know that your evolution is now in full activation mode! It's important to learn how to shut down your own psychic senses to keep "peeping Tom" psychics from voyeuristically reading your every thought. There are many privacy issues that have to be dealt with, as you will inevitably find out from your own psychic experiences.

I have touched on the most commonly experienced symptoms and signs of the empowering evolutionary shift into a world where higher frequencies will ignite all of your amazing abilities. Following is an easy "quick-start" reference list of some of the symptoms you may have as you "crown" into full awakening:

- ❈ Extreme fatigue and exhaustion.
- ❈ Interrupted sleep; waking up at night during certain times.
- ❈ Feelings of disorientation and confusion.
- ❈ Unexplained pain in your body, especially the chest, back, arms, legs, and feet.
- ❈ A noticeable change in your eating habits and a heightened sensitivity to preservatives.
- ❈ Food cravings, especially for salty foods.
- ❈ Weight gain, particularly in the abdominal area (the dreaded Buddha belly).

- Unexplained weight gain and an increased tendency to retain water.
- Chronic infections of the sinuses, ears, lungs, bladder, stomach, and intestines as you detox from all that negative energy.
- Dizziness, fainting, and even *petit mal* seizures as the brain adjusts to the higher frequencies and merging the left and right hemispheres.
- Headaches, especially between the eyes and at the crown of the head.
- Flu-like symptoms.
- Night sweats in both sexes, but not caused by menopause in women.
- Allergies, rashes, and unexplained bruises.
- Ringing and buzzing noises in the ears.
- Heart palpitations.
- Depression.
- Muscle contractions and cramping.
- Tingling in the arms, hands, feet, and top of head.
- Faster growth of hair and nails.
- Issues with short-term memory.
- Loss of concentration; often forgetting or searching for simple words.
- A more youthful appearance.
- Sudden discontent with spouse, partner, or friend.
- Feeling as though you're going crazy.
- Mood swings; extreme highs and lows as though you were bipolar.
- Anxiety and panic attacks.
- Self-sabotage that actually brings about necessary change.
- Decreased sex drive.

* Increased sensitivity to your environment (noise, crowds, smells).
* A wish to avoid other people.
* Changes in friends, hobbies, work, and/or residence.
* The feeling that time is moving quickly ("fast time").
* Increased spirituality; decreased interest in religious dogma.
* An awareness of psychic and telepathic abilities.

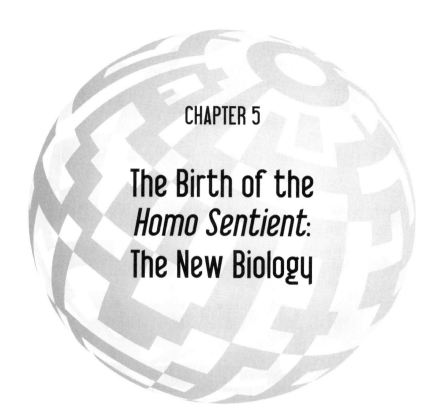

CHAPTER 5

The Birth of the *Homo Sentient:* The New Biology

This stage signals the arrival of the fully formed *Homo sentient*. This is what we have been waiting for as we endured the travails of the Quickening, Transition, and Crowning phases of the empowering shift. This new "upgrade" to our species will have bridged the mind, body, and spirit gaps. We will have a crystalline cellular structure as well as fully activated additional DNA strands. This new unified anatomy will completely alter how subjects such as biology, psychology, and, perhaps most of all, the true history of our planet are taught. We will now function as one unit, knowing that any imbalance in the mind, the physical body, or the spirit will have a direct and corresponding effect on the whole system. We are now a species that can lay claim to our birthright of higher consciousness.

What will happen if you choose *not* to ascend and keep shutting yourself off from the new frequencies coming into Earth's atmosphere?

> Should you choose to stay in three-dimensional consciousness, you may find yourself going in circles.

Should you choose to stay in three-dimensional consciousness—if you "abort" your evolution—you may find yourself spinning your wheels and going in circles, doing the same things over and over again and reaping the same results. This is akin to doing a complex math problem longhand while everyone else is using a calculator: You may come up with the same answer, but it will take you much longer to get it. Unfortunately there is bound to be a faction of society that will remain *Homo sentient*–phobic and prefer to let false beliefs and dogma dictate their lives instead of living authentically. If you choose to keep shutting down your abilities, eventually your whole vibration will suffer as you see others around you advance into a world where consciousness supersedes all of the material things that once seemed so important. You will truly be left behind.

This chapter will tell you how your psychic capabilities will be activated once the extra strands of your DNA are tuned to the higher channels of spirituality. You will learn about the importance of the pineal gland, the third eye, and how it works in tandem with the pituitary gland to bring about some of your most provocative and amazing psychic experiences. These two glands will function together as our psychic motherboard, connecting us to the light and new frequencies coming in. This light will begin the awakening and recoding process for our once-dormant DNA. The pineal gland is the feminine/receptive essence, and the pituitary gland is the masculine/active essence. Together they hold the key to balancing male and female energies, the physical and the spiritual.

Let's start with some new and interesting facts about the various properties of your DNA and its connection to the higher dimensions of consciousness.

The Cosmic-ology of DNA: Suddenly Psychic

In case you've forgotten what your high school biology class taught you about DNA, here is a bit of a primer to refresh your memory. This will help you get a better grasp on how your DNA is changing and connecting you to the new consciousness of higher dimensions. DNA stands for *deoxy-ribonucleic acid*, a nucleic acid that carries our genetic code in every cell of our body. DNA consists of two long chains of nucleotides twisted into a double helix and joined by hydrogen bonds between the complementary bases adenine (A) and thymine (T), or cytosine (C) and guanine (G). The sequence of nucleotides determines our individual hereditary characteristics such as eye color, height, and the shape of our nose. A gene is a distinct portion of a cell's DNA, and contains coded instructions for making everything the body needs. Genes are packaged in bundles called chromosomes. Most people have 23 pairs of chromosomes, yielding a total of 46. Each chromosome is made of protein and a single molecule of deoxy-ribonucleic acid (DNA). The genome is the entirety of your hereditary information. The genome includes both the genes and the non-coding sequences of DNA/RNA.

Now here is where it gets interesting: It is thought that only 10 percent of our entire DNA is actually used for the coding and reproduction of proteins; the rest is thought to be "junk" DNA. However, the Russian branch of the Human Genome Project, headed by Dr. Pjotr Garjajev, has actually uncovered the linguistic and psychic capabilities of this "junk" DNA, showing how it can actually be reprogrammed by words and frequencies. This proved that exposure to energy frequencies has a direct, measurable effect on our most (seemingly) immutable characteristics. With this information we can now crack the genetic code to gain access to our higher selves. The influx of supercharged frequencies that is jump-starting the evolutionary shift is causing our "junk" DNA to release the codes for our extrasensory capabilities.

> Exposure to energy frequencies has a direct, measurable effect on our most (seemingly) immutable characteristics.

We must adapt to expanding consciousness, faster frequencies, and the Divine order of the cosmos.

This is nothing new. Mystics have always known that sound can alter consciousness. The beautiful Gregorian chants that we find so mesmerizing contain *Solfeggio frequencies*, which are known to start the ascension process. Chanting, repetitive words, drumming, and even aromatic frequencies from incense and oils were the magick of the wise ones who had to artificially raise their vibrations to unlock the secret codes in their DNA. Fortunately this empowering frequency is available to all of us now, because our planet is optimally positioned to receive the new wave of energy that is enabling our next phase of evolution. So here we are, the *Homo sentients*, a far cry from the Neanderthal. We were pre-wired to evolve all along. That "junk" DNA isn't really junk at all: It was merely waiting to be activated when the time—and frequency—was right. Common wisdom dictates that that which does not change will die; we, too, must accommodate and adapt to expanding consciousness, faster frequencies, and the Divine order of the cosmos.

The new human biology is quantum biology, because those extra strands of our DNA are now connected to the universal consciousness, enabling us to become one with our spirit, our multidimensional, lighter body. We were taught to believe that double-strand DNA is the only formula for humanity. Guess again! This activation of our DNA will take us far beyond the mere physical blueprint that is coded in those two strands of protein and 46 chromosomes. With the help of those beautiful new waves and frequencies, your awakened *12-strand DNA* will yield a crystalline biology and a multidimensional consciousness of spiritual light and energy. The first pair of DNA strands codes to physical imprints, and the other five pairs of strands code to nonphysical energy imprints in the human energy field that are similar to a hologram. Future steps in our evolution may eventually activate as many as 24 DNA strands, which will enable us to realize our maximum potential as Divine beings.

Get ready for a futuristic, sci-fi world that you never thought possible. Clairvoyance, telekinesis, astral travel, telepathy, clairaudience, and clairsentience will be ordinary, everyday events. Phones will be obsolete because we'll be able to hear what someone is saying to us (and about us) just by tuning in with our thoughts. Who knows—someday we may even be able to download and stream music without the use of any devices. Your personal sense of reality will be dramatically altered after you evolve and shift into the new frequency. As well, your heightened sensitivity will engender a strong desire for peace and harmony, and make it much easier for you to understand and make sense of the changes you were obliged to make during the previous two evolutionary stages. All in all, this is a very inspired time for the planet and for the human race, the evolved *Homo sentient.*

The Pineal Portal

Flashes of psychic insight (psychic "hits"), remote viewing, and out-of-body experiences are sure to make you wonder what's going on. How can you get used to these newly activated extrasensory senses (beyond the five physical senses), especially if you were never really educated about how the subtle body functions above the physical body? Initially, psychic "hits," such as knowing what someone will say before he or she says it, or sensing that something is going to happen before it occurs, may be difficult to recognize and feel comfortable with. As you grow more accustomed to using these senses, however, these "hits" will come more frequently—and more easily.

Mystics and esoteric teachers have long known that the pineal gland, a tiny, cone-shaped gland situated in the center of the brain, is the connecting link between the physical and spiritual worlds. The pineal gland is often called the brain within the brain, but its physiological function has been largely unknown until recently. This little gland actually functions as the portal for your inner vision. In order to activate the third eye and perceive higher dimensions, the pineal gland and the pituitary gland (situated at the base of the brain) must vibrate in unison. The only way this can happen is if they are set to the right frequency. This can be achieved through meditation and relaxation techniques. When these two glands work together, flashes of intuition and psychic "hits" will come with increasing frequency. The pineal gland pulls in light/energy through the Crown chakra, located on top of the head, and then transfers it to the pituitary gland, which in turn disseminates it throughout your entire physical body. Because you are now being exposed to much higher frequencies, the pineal gland is able to open up quite naturally. The secrets of the sages and mystics, who opened their pineal glands through the practice of deep meditation and yoga, have now become accessible and completely natural for us. (Meditation and relaxation still remain beneficial practices to keep the third eye awake and tuned in, however.)

You only need look at ancient art and symbolism to see that the powers of the pineal gland have been known to humanity for ages. Pine cones, which represent the pineal gland, have often been used as symbols for enlightenment. The Staff of Osiris, who was the Egyptian god of life, death, fertility, and the underworld, bears a pine cone surrounded by the two serpents of the Kundalini, the life force that resides at the base of the spine. The staff represents the human spine, the snakes are the coiled energy that moves up toward the pine cone, and the pine cone itself represents the all-seeing third eye. There is a huge pine cone statue located at the Vatican in the Court of the Pigna (pine cone), and also one on the staff of the Pope. Pine cones appear frequently in religious paintings and images. In Genesis 32:30–31 in the Bible, Jacob wrestles all night with an angel and then names the place Peniel (a homologue of *pineal*), which means "face of God": "And Jacob called the name of the place Peniel: 'For I have seen God face to face, and my life is preserved.' And as he passed over Penuel [a variant of Peniel] the sun rose upon him." Could this mean that Jacob connected with his third eye and filled his body with light/enlightenment, thereby connecting to the Divine? In Matthew 6:22, Jesus says, "If your eye be single your body will fill with light," another likely reference to the pineal gland.

Pine cones regularly appear framed in Freemason octagons on the ceilings of Masonic lodges, and a large Freemason sculpture on the side of the Whitehall Building in the New York Financial District depicts two intertwining snakes spiraling up to a pine cone. As well, the Freemasons' revered 33-degree mark represents the number of vertebrae on the human spinal cord. Freemasons seem to know the spiritual significance of the third eye and pay iconic tribute to it, even as they continue to hoodwink the public with their outwardly dogmatic stance.

When your pineal gland awakens, you may feel pressure at the base of your skull. This pressure will often occur when you are connecting to the frequencies of higher realms. A head injury can also activate the third eye. I believe this is what happened to me: When I was about 12 years old a horse I was riding threw me into a tree, and I definitely sensed something different about my perceptions after that incident. Of course, I also had one heck of a headache! The pineal gland is thought to generate the most powerful and highest source of ethereal energy available to us. It has always been important in initiating supernatural powers and developing psychic talents. Psychics who regularly use their third eye, the pineal gland, have finely honed capabilities because they exercise this natural function of the spirit so often. As we evolve spiritually, using this third eye will become as natural as using your physical eyes.

This gland also controls the various physiological rhythms of the body. It works in harmony with the hypothalamus gland, which regulates thirst, hunger, sexual desire, and the biological clock that determines how you age. The pineal gland also produces the hormone melatonin, which is secreted in the absence of light. Melatonin is probably the most efficient natural cell protection agent in your body, and is even more essential now that your DNA is coding to the new frequency from the empowering shift. There is evidence that melatonin slows the aging rate, improves mood, im-

> Using this third eye will become as natural as using your physical eyes.

proves skin health and appearance, increases intelligence, and makes you feel younger and rejuvenated. Now we know what is meant by "getting your beauty rest."

As you might imagine, the pineal gland is quite sensitive to electromagnetic energy. Studies show that there are calcite microcrystals in the pineal gland that are *piezoelectric*, meaning that they can turn one type of energy into another. These microcrystals pick up the new waves of energy coming into Earth's atmosphere and tune in to the realms of higher consciousness where telepathy, clairvoyance, and other psychic capabilities are possible. The pineal gland is also very sensitive to fluoride. Fluoride can cause calcification in the gland. (Think of it as having sand in your third eye.) If the pineal gland is impaired, you will not be able to effectively pick up the frequencies that link to enlightenment. Holistic medicine and energy medicine know how the frequency from a crystal can change the frequency within the body to transmute illness into a healing, and quartz crystals were often used in radios to pick up radio waves and signals. Our pineal crystals are the newest biotechnology for healing and communication. We can now tap into the collective consciousness the way that your computer connects to the World Wide Web.

Did you know that the pineal gland's melatonin production changes in response to the Earth's magnetic field and is closely correlated to geomagnetic latitude with respect to Earth's magnetic poles? Both human and animal circadian rhythms are driven by the day/night cycle and are synchronized with natural geomagnetic electromagnetic fields. There has been much debate whether the manmade electromagnetic frequency (EMF) from cell phones and computers really has an adverse effect on the pineal gland and reduces melatonin production. When you see flocks of birds dropping from the sky en masse, beached whales, dolphins dying, and schools of fish seemingly committing suicide, you have to wonder if manmade frequencies are causing these terrible things to happen.

There is some speculation that there is a conspiracy afoot to halt our psychic evolution via the use of EMF. HAARP (the High-frequency Active Auroral Research Program) in Alaska has been presented to the public as a study of the ionosphere. Its supposed purpose is to show how our communication systems can benefit by

> We can tap into the collective consciousness the way that your computer connects to the World Wide Web.

studying the way frequency waves (whether stimulated by artificial wave transmission or by natural transmission) bounce around the ionosphere, which owes its existence primarily to ultraviolet radiation from the sun. Could scientific manipulation of the frequency waves we are exposed to through our electronic gadgets and also through HAARP itself be a way for Big Brother to attempt to control, hinder, or even halt our evolution? Are you starting to see how the shift of the magnetic poles is also stimulating the pineal gland and causing a shift within your own energy field? Any changes in the sun's poles or Earth's poles will affect the magnetic field around the Earth as well as your personal frequency.

Out-of-Body Experiences

The pineal gland is your cosmic sensor. When activated, the pineal gland becomes the direct line of communication to the higher dimensions. Sometimes the vibration level of the extrasensory spirit body can be raised high enough to allow it to actually separate from the physical body. Many people have had experiences in which they thought they were dreaming and looking down on their body, when in actuality they were taking extrasensory baby steps with their cosmic essence, the spirit. It is now possible to have out-of-body experiences (OBEs) *at will* in order to work through parallel life issues that are still playing out above the physical plane. There, you can meet up with spirit guides, visit your other life incarnations, and fine-tune future life experiences. If you would like to have a willed out-of-body experience (as opposed to a spontaneous one), you must learn how to be physically relaxed but mentally alert. The way to achieve this is to get into a deep state of meditation and visualize your subtle body (your spirit) escaping through the "portal" of the pineal gland and out through the Crown chakra, located on top of your head. (Don't worry about dying or not being able to get back into your physical body; there is a psychic "umbilical cord" that anchors everyone's spirit to their physical form, and it only fully releases

> The pineal gland becomes the direct line of communication to the higher dimensions.

when your time to expire finally arrives.) People who have successfully mastered astral projection and OBEs often report hearing a popping or whooshing sound when their astral body separates from their physical body, so be prepared for that. Before the projection process is complete, your body may feel like a lead weight and you may be unable to move. Deep relaxation usually leads to state of temporary paralysis, but this is not something to resist or worry about; it will lead to an altered state of consciousness that is necessary for a successful OBE.

Before you attempt any astral travel, however, you should read through this book in its entirety. Become familiar with your extrasensory spirit and learn to be responsible in the use of your natural capabilities. It's also important to be aware of what you might find out there. If your vibration isn't high enough to get you to the fifth plane or the higher astral realm, you might find yourself in the lower astral plane. The lower plane is where negative, fragmented thought-forms, bizarre inhabitants, and confusion reign. It is your worst lucid nightmare come true. Some people have returned from an OBE in the foggy murk of the lower astral plane with reports of wrestling with evil entities. It is possible to physically manifest bruises on your body if your spirit encounters an energy attack in the lower astral level. Just as you have to learn to walk before you can run, so must you take your time learning to activate, appreciate, and protect your energetic essence.

You may already have had an out-of-body experience but thought you were just dreaming. Spontaneous out-of-body or astral projection usually occurs just prior to falling asleep or right before waking up, when the mind is awake but the body is still dormant. During an OBE you may feel as though you can't move, speak, or breathe. You may even feel as though you are tumbling or falling. Oftentimes a high-pitched sound accompanies these sensations. Fear usually sets in at that point, jolting you awake and shutting down the whole experience. But what would happen if you dropped the fear (which automatically lowers your vibration) and just went with the feeling, allowing yourself to feel excited about the prospect of astral travel? At first, like a tentative bird leaving its nest, you might not venture out very far. I remember one of my first OBEs. I was lying on the sofa in a state of semi-sleep but trying desperately to stay awake when I suddenly heard a high-pitched sound. The next thing I knew, I was standing off to the side of the room watching my daughter (who was 2 years old at the time) climb out of her playpen and proceed to take all of my books off the bookshelf. I willed myself to get back into my body and jumped up, wondering what had just happened. I immediately went over to the bookshelf, where I found my daughter, who was indeed out of her playpen and enthusiastically pulling all my books to the floor. I dismissed the experience as coincidence, but deep inside I knew that I had been out of my body because I was unable to move or talk, yet, I still possessed a strange kind of awareness as I looked at myself lying on the sofa and observed my environment.

When you go all the way out and actually project yourself to another location, the feeling is unmistakable. The first time I really let myself go and didn't fight the feeling of sleep paralysis is actually what convinced me that we really do possess the ability to roam the higher dimensions and exist beyond the physical realms. It was 1994, and I can still remember the sound of what seemed to be a loud sonic boom and then suddenly finding myself on a sunny street lined with extremely tall palm trees. I had no idea where I was as I walked into the lobby of a big building with elevators to my left and a round receptionist's desk in the middle. I approached the woman behind the desk and, before I uttered a word, she told me in a matter-of-fact manner that Raul Julia had just died. I walked back outside and suddenly felt myself floating and sliding back into my body as though I were on a water slide. I woke up feeling as though I had just experienced something that was definitely *not* a dream. I didn't even know who Raul Julia was.

The next day I was getting the kids ready for school when I heard a reporter on the morning news say that there was some sad news in from Los Angeles: Raul Julia had died. I nearly died, too, because there was that name. *Who is this guy?* I wondered. The news reporter said that Raul Julia was an actor who had been in the very popular movie *The Addams Family* and many other films and television shows. I ran to where my kids kept their video collection and pulled out the movie; I had to see what he looked like. Why and how did I know about his death 24 hours or more before it oc-curred? I figured if anyone could explain this crazy situation to me, it would be a Native American friend of mine who was a practicing shaman. She told me this had happened so that I would be convinced of the reality of OBEs. She told me that I had shifted into a higher consciousness and that I should expect more experiences like that one in the future. I would learn how to work outside of my body to help heal wounds from prior incarnations and also work with spirit guides to retrieve information that could be helpful to me and others. When she told me all of this I realized that we are only confined by the limits of our mind, not by physical walls, and I had my pineal gland to thank for it.

> We are only confined by the limits of our mind, not by physical walls.

Making Sense of Your New Senses

If you were born during or after the late 1980s you probably already knew that you had these gifts. The rest of us who were born prior to that time are just beginning to open up to our spiritual nature. When your psychic senses first start to kick in you may feel a little confused and un-settled. Just as a baby learns about her environment through her physical senses, you, too, will learn about your world of frequency by recogniz-ing how energy feels, tastes, and sounds. You will learn how to decode the messages embedded in your psychic "hits," synchronicities, dreams, out-of-body experiences, and other psi experiences. Your heightened ad-ditional senses will also enable you to be more discerning in the choices you make. Imagine standing on a rooftop and being able to see the en-tire city below you; much different than being on the ground, isn't it?

Psychically speaking, you will be released from the three-dimensional box and able to look at things from a higher perspective. You will enjoy the best of both worlds: spiritual and material.

A New Origin of Our Species

So where did we get our extrasensory genetic makeup in the first place? The big mystery of the ages that has been encoded in sacred texts and hidden away in such places as the Vatican Library tells us where the original humans, the designer species, came from—"designer" because our creation was not an accident of natural evolution. As was recorded in these historical texts (which are now finally coming to light because of the empowering shift), we have an alien heritage.

The cross is generally seen as a religious symbol, but its real purpose is to symbolize the hybridization (crossing, if you will) of man's genetic material with the genes of our ancient ancestors, the gods of old. These were Earth's first conquerors, aliens from Nibiru and other star systems. Despite what Darwin asserted, we did not accidentally evolve from apes. Even Francis Crick, the English physicist, molecular biologist, and neuroscientist who was one of the co-discoverer of the structure of DNA, didn't believe that the DNA molecule could have developed in only 500 or 600 million years by accident. He, too, speculated that we are a hybrid of an earthly and an alien species.

The true story of our ancestry was encoded and buried within myths and religious narratives that fell prey to the "telephone effect," which warped and manipulated the information to fit into certain belief systems. If you look closely, however, you can see unifying clues to the truth. For example, DNA manipulation or alien genetic hybridization (the splicing of human DNA with alien DNA) is actually described in certain passages in the Bible—in Genesis 1:26, for instance: "And God said let *us* make man in *our* image, after our likeness." The original Hebrew translation reads quite

> We are a hybrid of an earthly and an alien species.

differently: "And the *Gods* said, let us *remake* man in our image after our likeness." Notice the use of the plural and the word *remake*. This implies that previous attempts had been made to create a hybrid race before we were, in essence, remade (that is, genetically modified).

To make a very long history short, here is how the human race as we know it today really came about. The first rulers of this planet were the Anunnaki from Nibiru, the planet of the crossing. *Anunnaki* is a Sumerian word meaning "those who from heaven to earth came." These alien-gods came to earth to mine gold in order to protect their own planet from the same solar radiation that is currently threatening our planet. The Anunnaki were the *Elohim* ("gods") who made us in their image. Their intention was the creation of a slave labor caste, a sub-Annunaki race, that would mine the gold they needed. The lower-echelon Annunaki refused to do physical work and rebelled against the conditions in the mines. Enki, their chief scientist, along with his half-sister, Ninhursag, their chief medical officer, were commissioned by the council of the gods to fashion a worker race through the use of genetic manipulation. They were obliged to make and remake this new race several times after initially getting unsatisfactory results from splicing animal genes with the already-existing *Homo erectus*. Eventually they merged their alien genes with those of *Homo erectus*, thus giving birth to *Homo sapiens*. We were not the result of a process of evolution but a solution to a problem. Ninhursag carried the first of these mixed-race beings to term, giving birth to a being she called the "Lulu." Later, birth goddesses (female Anunnaki) produced additional workers. Because a hybrid is incapable of procreation (just as the mule, a cross between horse and donkey, cannot reproduce itself), this process was not sustainable. Enki decided to take matters into his own hands and cohabitate with one of these hybrids without the consent of his half-brother, Enlil, the chief god. Their resulting progeny produced a species with enhanced DNA and upgraded consciousness that was able to replicate itself. Indeed, in Genesis 6 we read that the *sons* of the gods mated with human females. This was not supposed to happen, but it did.

The offspring of this union were godlike in that they now had the ability to surmount and transcend the primal instincts of the original

Homo erectus. Eventually this race reproduced more precociously than the Anunnaki had perhaps anticipated. A dispute then arose among the gods as to the morality of keeping humans as slaves. One group approved; another did not. This created a rift between the ruling Elohim. In the Book of Enoch (Enoch was the great-grandfather of Noah), we also learn of the so-called fallen angels (emissaries or messengers) who mated with humans and taught them many scientific and occult skills. Our family tree contains many occultists, builders, scientists, and even makeup artists. You can see from the following ancient ancestry genealogy recorded in the Book of Enoch how we were taught the magick of the cosmos:

- Armaros taught humanity the resolving of enchantments and root cutting (herbology and spells).
- Araqiel taught humans the signs of the earth.
- Azazel taught humans to make knives, swords, and shields. He also taught them how to devise ornaments and cosmetics.
- Baraqel taught humanity astrology.
- Chazaqiel taught us the signs of the clouds (meteorology).
- Kokabiel was a high-ranking being who commanded 365,000 surrogate spirits to do his bidding. He also instructed his fellows in astrology.
- Sariel, one of the seven archangels, originally listed as Saraqel, taught the courses of the moon (at one time regarded as forbidden knowledge).
- Shamsiel, once a guardian of Eden, was the head of 365 legions of angels. He also had the power and authority to accompany prayers to the fifth dimension (heaven). In Enoch I he is a fallen angel who teaches the signs of the sun.

The growing licentiousness of Earth's new inhabitants so irritated Enlil that he decided not to alert them to an impending catastrophic flood. Enki, however, forewarned Noah, a man whose bloodline was thought to be less corrupt than the rest of humanity, and instructed him to build an ark to save his family and "the seed of all living things."

Could this "seed" refer to DNA? Today, on the Arctic island of Svalbard, there is a vault that stores the seeds of hundreds of thousands of plants in case of global catastrophe.

The time of the global flood has been set at approximately 9500 BC. It is not until 3800 BC that the culture of the Sumerians shows up, seemingly having no precursor. Once again the gods made an appearance, this time trying to fix the mess that they themselves created. That particular story is outlined in the Old Testament, starting with Abraham of Ur, a city that was located in modern-day Iraq. The majority of the Anunnaki left our planet sometime around 500 BC, but it is believed that some remained. This is why anthropologists still have not been able to identify that missing link, the dynamic precursor to explain the radical departure from the first hominoid to our present advanced state, which supposedly took place in the space of only 500,000 years.

The Anunnaki feared that someday the servant (humanity) would become the master. Their main blunder was tempting humanity with knowledge—celestial knowledge/astrology, advanced technology, telepathy, shape-shifting, astral travel, medical knowledge—when humanity was not intelligent or sophisticated enough to integrate this knowledge into their lives and use it responsibly. (Think of it as encouraging underage drinking, but on a celestial level.) They realized that the primal instincts of *Homo erectus*, combined with the powers of their advanced, alien genetic code, could produce a species capable of causing problems for all the surrounding galactic communities.

> Vibrations from a fear-based consciousness will lower your overall vibration.

As you will remember from previous chapters, the vibrations from a fear-based consciousness will lower your overall vibration, in essence keeping you from connecting to enlightenment and higher consciousness. Our newly attained consciousness of spirit became a license for oppressive religious and political ideologies to take root. Such ideologies were apparently designed to undermine our evolution and self-knowledge—in other words, our power. Imagine growing up thinking that you were poor, only to find out one day that you were really rich, and that you had been purposefully misled so that others could control you and your money. This is similar to what happened to us on a cosmic scale. The Anunnaki were not the only members of the galactic community to manipulate an earthly species, but they were the primary players who initially instigated the process. This is why the empowering shift is such a critical time for Earth and her inhabitants. We are just now evolving into our full genetic capabilities, and only the collective consciousness attuned to the highest vibrations of love will enable us to grow responsibly into our highest good. The other galactic communities in the universe have always known that a time would come when our evolution would surpass our technology.

> We are all created equal, and we all come from the one true Source.

Alien intervention is still going on today. Given how we have treated our planet throughout the centuries, the remaining Anunnaki are afraid that we will jeopardize Earth's ascension. If we continue to operate from the lower vibrations and—worst-case scenario—nuke ourselves into oblivion, we also jeopardize the well-being of the entire galactic community. Can you imagine what would happen if, for instance, we lost one of the planets in our solar system? It would throw off the gravitational pull and vibration of every other planet and wreak havoc in the heavens. It could be the end of our galaxy as we know it. Fortunately, we now have the chance to reclaim our lost genetic heritage and use it for the highest good of all. We are all created equal, and we all come from the one true Source. Once we drop the fear and false beliefs, we will find union with each other, with our planet, and with the Divine.

The next chapter will familiarize you with some setbacks and problems you may encounter as you use your newly activated senses. Privacy issues, manipulation, psychic bullies, and psychic vampires are all part and parcel of becoming fully *Homo sentient*. Fortunately there is much you can do to care for and protect these new senses. Read on to find out how.

CHAPTER 6

Baby Steps:
The Care and Feeding of the
Homo Sentient

Charles Darwin once said that "It is not the strongest of the species that survive, nor the most intelligent, but the one most responsive to change." With your changed consciousness, being psychic is now just as natural and normal as breathing. Now that you are a fully fledged *Homo sentient*, you need to learn how to nurture and use your gifts responsibly and, if necessary, protect them and yourself from danger, intruders, or just plain nuisances. Much of this will be trial and error on your part, but I can give you some helpful tips to get you started on the right foot. The two basic frequencies from which everything is derived (and that drive us) are love and fear. Your new task will be to constantly calibrate and recalibrate these two emotional charges and try to always pull in the highest vibration to ensure that your physical,

> Being psychic is now just as natural and normal as breathing.

> The two basic frequencies from which everything is derived (and which drive us) are love and fear.

emotional, and spiritual well-being can merge successfully into one unified vibration. Keep in mind that fear always gives birth to hate, and hate is like kryptonite to your evolving self. It blocks empathy and compassion, and tends to breed the negative vibrations of apathy, jealousy, greed, arrogance, criticism, separateness, and cruelty. Therefore, some of this process will involve transmuting negative energy into more neutral vibrations.

Your surroundings will always hold an energy imprint from everything that has occurred there. With your new abilities, you will learn to adjust your own vibration to these imprints intuitively and automatically, the same way that a sound engineer knows how to mix the right balance of sound frequencies to produce the best possible recording. It is actually your chakra centers that will clue you in to these frequencies, and enable you to safeguard your abilities, if necessary. You will learn to tell the difference between positive and negative energy by being more aware of how things feel vibrationally. Your chakras will signal you with a familiar feeling that you will then associate with a corresponding emotion. Your intuition will help you be even more discriminating. Just as everyone has his or her own personal style, you will develop your own distinct style of psychic sensing. Likewise, the energy from your own aura will alert others as to your true thoughts, feelings, and intentions; without your uttering a single word, your authentic self will be exposed to those who have eyes to see. (Imagine how this will change the landscape of politics and religion!) You are detaching from the old, structured beliefs and the false illusion of materialism and advancing toward a new consciousness of spirituality and energy. As you adjust to your transformation, living your truth will be your new mantra.

> Fear always gives birth to hate, and hate is like kryptonite to your evolving self.

Because you are now so sensitive to frequency of any kind, anything too heavy or negative can upset your highly sensitive psychic senses. Animals have always been sensitive to the vibrations around them as a means of survival; it is said that birds would not sing near Belsen and Dachau, the infamous Nazi concentration camps. They likely could not resonate with all of the negative vibrations emanating from those terrible places. Even the cells in your body communicate with each other via frequency signals. Your psychic senses respond to ambient frequencies in the same way and connect what is registered by your subtle body to your physical body to give you enhanced perception beyond the five physical senses. Once you receive these frequencies, they are accepted, through transduction, as energy in one form, processed as energy in a different form, and finally realized in the form of action. What all of this means is you are naturally "tuned" to be psychic.

Maintaining a sufficiently high personal vibration is vital because the energy from your thoughts, which affects you on an individual level, can go out into the ether and spread like a virus throughout the collective consciousness. No man or woman is an island. Don't forget that your newly activated DNA will dramatically magnify and quicken the manifestation of your thoughts and desires, so always be cognizant of your intentions. If you remember back in Chapter 1, staying in the moment is what lays the groundwork for your creative visualizations; it is what enables them to manifest. You imagine it, sense it, feel it, and *know* what form it will take before it materializes because you are now working with energy that is sourced from a higher plane of consciousness. You tune in to the universal language of frequency around you through awareness, by looking for numerical and synchronistic signals, and by listening to your augmented psychic senses. A well-maintained and carefully protected personal frequency will give you the following benefits:

> Maintaining a sufficiently high personal vibration is vital.

❀ Increased ability to access sacred knowledge and open up to your inner gifts of knowing, sensing, seeing, and hearing.

❀ Greater awareness and expanded consciousness.

❀ Expanded ability to experience unconditional love.

❀ A body that feels and looks younger.

❀ Increased psychic abilities and self-trust.

❀ Improved eyesight and psychic seeing.

❀ Detoxification on the emotional and physical levels.

❀ Increased energy and improved memory.

❀ Increased inner peace and calmness.

❀ Better connection to the spirit realms.

❀ Better understanding of one's life journey.

❀ Clearing of limiting beliefs and patterns, some that may have been held for several lifetimes.

❀ Reduction of fear and doubt.

❀ Deep emotional release.

❀ Clearer insight about everything.

❀ Resolution of relationship difficulties.

❀ Ability to self-diagnose, heal, and more easily let go of painful patterns.

Conversely, a neglected and vulnerable personal frequency has quite a few drawbacks (I prefer to call them challenges). These include:

❀ Increased sensitivity to energy, sometimes to the point of feeling overloaded and/or paranoid.

❀ Lack of privacy, as others can now clearly sense your intentions.

❀ Increased vulnerability to psychic vampires and attacks.

❀ Taking on the physical and emotional pain of others via increased empathy.

❀ Psychic burnout from being too open.

❋ Headaches, especially on the crown of the head and behind the eyes, that increase in severity and duration when dealing with heavy or negative energy.

❋ Vulnerability to errant, trickster energies and the psychic flu/ energy viruses.

❋ Frequent malfunction of electrical devices from being ungrounded and unbalanced.

With Power Comes Responsibility

Your ability to manifest is much more marked at this stage of your evolution because the frequencies from the Galactic Center are integrating your mind with the creative qualities of your spirit essence. Your enhanced DNA now enables an almost instantaneous manifestation of your thoughts. As you would with any creation, you need to be responsible with your thought life, because thought vibrations eventually slow down enough to take on actual form. (This idea is akin to watching a top spinning: It's impossible to really see it until it slows down enough for you to see its form, as opposed to the blur of whirling energy.) The frequencies of words can be slowed down enough to turn into matter as well. Sound has amazing creative capabilities. Chanting, singing, drumming, rattling, and prayer are but a few examples of how repeated vibrations build up an intense energy that can link up with your thought waves and alter reality. When you are exposed to higher vibrations, your "psychic wiring" will recalibrate to match up with corresponding frequencies and manifest a created reality. Do you see why it is important to hang out with the right crowd? The lower energy that comes from angry, fearful, or malcontented people will affect your own energy levels. You may even feel physically ill when you are

> *Your enhanced DNA now enables an almost-instantaneous manifestation of your thoughts.*

> *Sound has amazing creative capabilities.*

around such people. Eventually you will find that you no longer wish to engage with the lower energy that once kept you trapped in unnecessary, self-created drama. You will also be able to sail through problems once you realize that they are just an illusion of the third dimension. You will be able to transcend that realm to actively create, recalibrate, and transmute any energy that isn't right for you. It all starts with your thoughts. They are your blueprints for tomorrow.

Be aware that attachment to a specific outcome will limit your choices. Be open to all possible outcomes because you may wind up with an even better resolution than you had imagined. There are no set formulas or specific guidelines for manifesting, because everyone seems to find their own creative method that best helps them create their desired reality. However, staying in the moment of intention is always important when you are syncing up your energy with the vibrations around you. At this stage you are now open to your empowerment—the sacred geometry of chance, the Divine order of the universe that holds the fortuitous elements of existence that wondrously manifest as your created reality.

If you wish to manifest something, your thoughts, working in conjunction with your imagination, will always produce the desired results. *But what about horrendous life situations?* you may ask. *Why would anyone create pain and suffering for themselves? Are they masochists? Or are they just being irresponsible?* Neither, actually. Unfavorable situations are typically summoned through fragmented thought-forms created out of fear and the constant replay of hurts and traumas. These fragmented thought-forms also increase one's chances of attracting negative entities. And of course there are always unevolved, irresponsible, or downright malevolent people who will manipulate energy and/or entities with the intention of causing you harm. The upside to all of this is that your enhanced extrasensory senses will enable you to pick up on any errant negative energy before it reaches you.

> You are now open to your empowerment.

Keeping Your Vibrations High

You must also be vigilant about maintaining your vibration at a high enough level to enable you to navigate through life more purposefully, authentically, and, most importantly, safely. You will attract whatever you imagine, so to be mindful of the frequencies you are focusing on. Living in "fast time," as opposed to linear time, means that events unfold much more quickly, so be mindful that you don't inadvertently bring about an unwanted situation simply by letting your frequency diminish. Yes, you are psychically attuned and evolved enough to create whatever you wish, but please—no manipulation of anyone's free will, as nothing will diminish your energy more quickly. Keep your vibrations high or risk dissolving instead of evolving. You can maintain a high vibration level by:

❋ Releasing all energy vibrations from shame, blame, or guilt.

❋ Refusing victim consciousness.

❋ Cutting any energy cords that are draining you.

❋ Grounding your energy through meditation and relaxation.

❋ Removing emotional blockages through regression therapy and Reiki.

❋ Protecting yourself by visualizing a white light around you.

❋ Removing yourself from drama and chaos.

❋ Being selective regarding whom you invite into your space.

Not taking things personally also helps. Be the observer; don't let yourself get hooked into any drama. As we experience these mental, emotional, and physical changes, we may notice that others around us are treading water or are even resentful of the new us. The reason for this is that they are still living in the old world of duality and control. Again, don't take it personally.

Your overall vibration level determines your world and how you experience it. When you are feeling down and your vibration bottoms out, your perception of reality will be negative. You also may find it difficult to relate to someone who is having a stroke of good luck because you

Recalibrate your frequency by linking up to the love vibration.

aren't tuned in to that frequency. The best way to get out of the dumps is to recalibrate your frequency by linking up to the love vibration. Yes, love has a vibration! It's precisely 528 Hz, a frequency that stimulates creativity, benefits the heart, and brings about almost-instantaneous manifestation. Love raises your vibrations, taking them from dense, slow frequencies to faster, finer frequencies. Higher vibrations enable you to let in more light; suddenly, things will appear to come about for your highest good and the good of the collective consciousness. Have you ever noticed how people who are in love always seem to lose weight and look their best? This happens because they are vibrating at a high level and becoming lighter, spiritually speaking. The love frequency is even capable of bringing about miracles when it is resonating with a well-intended, visualized thoughtform. This is actually what occurs during healings. The use of imagery changes the vibrations of the body on a cellular level. When that imagery is reinforced and confirmed with a driving positive intention behind it, a miracle often results. Love comes from the heart, not the ego, and when you work with love energy you are drawing on the main voltage line of the Divine.

In the previous three stages of your evolution, you went through the purging of negative attachments trapped in your aura and subtle body so that you could cut any emotional cords attached to unhealthy relationships and negative memories. You must now fill the void with something positive. (Remember that nature abhors a vacuum.) Always fill up those spaces with light: Take a few purposeful, deep breaths and visualize your whole body and surrounding aura filling up with white light to ensure that you attract higher vibrations into your essence. One of the hardest lessons in life is learning to let go. Created drama will keep you stuck as you continuously attract more of the same vibration. Remember that you can also transmute negative energy. Don't dwell on problems; your time is better spent thinking up positive solutions to your dilemmas so that you can move forward. Every time you look back and obsess over something, you reset yourself back to Day One. The solution is simple:

Put down those limited (and limiting) patterns of behavior that you've been carrying. You will feel so much lighter for it.

Navigating Relationships

You already know that you leave energetic "fingerprints," or residue, on things that you have touched and places you have been. You also know that you have a direct and measurable effect on the energy of others, just as you are affected by their energy in turn. Our relationships with others will be light-years better when there is mutual awareness of shared parallel/past lives, and when all karma and negative emotional ties have been resolved. Relationships are also much more authentic because your extrasensory senses will let you know when something is amiss; even the most accomplished liars and spin doctors won't be able to circumvent these abilities. What used to be at least a seven-second window to glean a first impression has become a mere nanosecond now that we have access to our extrasensory senses. Prior to the energy shift most first impressions were formed based on appearance, body language, and, if you were lucky, a hunch or gut feeling. Now, however, you can size someone up simply by tuning in to the vibrations you pick up from his or her name or voice. Pay attention to handshakes, too. The exchange of energy can be very telling for both people. Frequency really is a kind of fingerprinting that helps us identify people and their intentions. As you shift into higher consciousness, you will meet more and more people who will seem very familiar to you. This is almost always the result of a shared energy imprint from another experienced life. The fact is that we usually incarnate within the same spirit group or groups so we can work as a team in correcting the collective consciousness while helping our planet ascend and evolve along with us.

> You can size someone up simply by tuning in to the vibrations you pick up from his or her name or voice.

Protective Measures

Personal privacy and protection of your newly expanded psychic abilities are vital. Even your most private thoughts and ideas can now be picked up psychically by someone, leaving you vulnerable to frequency hackers. Frequency hackers are people who have not yet learned the proper psychic etiquette; either by accident or intentionally, they somehow manage to tune in to someone else's personal channel. Likewise, you should not go into anyone else's energy zone uninvited. But what about the cases in which you unintentionally pick up on someone's frequency and learn something about him or her clairvoyantly? What is the protocol? First, determine if what you are seeing is for your or their highest good. If it is, you may allow yourself to continue picking up the psychic impressions. If you should unintentionally pick up on someone's private business, however, the best thing to do is to blink repeatedly for a few seconds. This will serve to delete the accidental "download." Then, release what you've already picked up—unless, of course, it is information you are supposed to have. You'll intuitively know the difference once you get used to the process.

Defensive Tactics

Just as your computer needs a firewall and virus protection installed, you will need some protective and defensive tactics in your energetic arsenal. Being too psychically open can put you right in the path of psychic saboteurs, energy vampires, and telepathic peeping Toms. The proper protective measures will help defend you against the fragmented spirits of the dead, negative thought-forms, and ambient emotional energies in the etheric, astral, and lower mental planes. The last thing you need is a negative thought-form possessing your subtle body. Let's start with what you can do to ensure that your energetic boundaries are safe. First of all, grounding is of the utmost importance. Imagine you are hardwiring a light in your home: You have the red, or "hot," wire and the white, or "neutral," wire. If there is no ground wire, however, sparks and shorting out will result. The same goes for your energetic makeup: You need to be grounded and balanced in order for your psychic senses to operate properly.

The most common way to ground your energy is to imagine that you are dropping roots deep into the ground and feeling firmly anchored to the earth. This prevents any negative frequencies from attaching themselves to you. Instead, they will pass into the earth, fracture, and dissipate. Once you have dropped your grounding roots, visualize a protective, white bubble around yourself; this acts as a barrier against psychic saboteurs. If you feel you are under psychic attack, shield yourself by visualizing a wall of mirrors surrounding you; this will reflect any negativity back to its source. It is also very common to have things break, especially electrical items, when you are around someone who is intruding on, harming, or feeding on your frequency. Some people are, quite literally, hot-wired for drama.

In some instances you may unknowingly attract parasitic energy vampires who try to attach themselves to your light. These energy vampires piggyback on your energy and drain you emotionally. This is the needy friend who has no idea he or she is siphoning the life out of you. Stressful situations are also a form of vampirism because they drain you of your *chi*, or life force, leaving you feeling depressed and tired. Oppressive governments, exploitative companies, bad relationships, dead-end jobs, and negative news stories all fall under the category of energy zappers. If a certain person or situation keeps you feeling exhausted, depressed, and depleted, you are probably dealing with an energy vampire. Energy vampires are not always aware of what they are doing, and they may not know they're harming you. Sometimes they do it by keeping up a steady stream of exhausting small talk, or by dumping all of their problems on you. These types of people often expect you to help fix them at the expense of your own energy and health. These people are so ungrounded that they are forced to attach to a host—you—and basically take you for everything you've got.

Should you ever come across an energy vampire (and chances are you will), make sure you clean up any energy residue afterward. For example, if this kind of person has been in your home or office, he or she will often leave a trail of negative vibes behind. You can clear out the leftover energy by burning some white sage or sprinkling sea salt in the corners of the room. Always make sure to get the corners of the room because that is where energy seems to collect. An even easier method to clear out negative energy is to imagine yourself sweeping the energy out the door and then mentally shooting a beam of white light around the room (again, don't forget the corners). Finally, you must enforce energy boundaries, meaning that you must know when to pull back from such a person. "Closed" body language—for example, crossing your arms in front of you or crossing your legs at the ankles—is a simple way to impede any potential parasites. Retract your aura and take notice of any signals coming from your chakras; are they trying to tell you something more?

Many cultures believe that it is possible to open the Third Eye chakra, the pineal portal, for negative purposes such as psychic attack. This is called the evil eye (the *malocchio*). The idea of giving someone the evil eye stems from the fact that we all have a third eye. All it takes is an unsettling, malevolent stare that lasts too long. Envious and jealous thoughts can put the *malocchio* on the intended target. Powerful thought-forms directed at an unknowing victim can wreak havoc in his or her life. Some of the symptoms of this kind of psychic attack are depression, nightmares, chronic health problems, headaches, ongoing bad luck, and, in extreme instances, the manifestation of strange, foul odors. Remember to always be vigilant about the type of energy that you draw to yourself. We no longer fight our battles with sticks, stones, guns, or knives because we have something much more lethal: energy.

> We no longer fight our battles with sticks, stones, guns, or knives because we have something much more lethal—energy.

If you feel that someone has attacked you in any way, the first thing you should do is create a wall of protection around yourself. This in itself is a very powerful thought-form. Before you go out, imagine that your third eye is covered by something that looks like a small pocket mirror;

this will serve the purpose of reflecting any negativity back to the sender. Then, beam a strong white light around yourself, close all of your "hatches" (chakras), and imagine yourself levitating above any intrusive or harmful energy. The lower vibrations from negativity will not be able to sustain themselves for very long unless you engage them and feed them some of your own vital energy. This is an imaginative process, but remember that consciousness comes first and that, whatever you think, you can manifest.

Food, Medication, and Other Factors

In order to maintain and protect your newly opened extrasensory senses, you'll need to be vigilant about the frequencies of the foods you eat. Food is fuel for the physical body, but it is also much more than that. The vibrations of foods directly affect your psychic centers. You know what happens if you download a lot of useless crap on your computer: It will crash. Low-octane fuel will cause a car to sputter and set off your "check engine" light. Likewise, food with negative energy or lower vibrations can cause problems in your subtle body system, which in turn may hinder your evolution. Processed foods, additives, dyes, hormones, and medications are all likely culprits. This is the problem that the energy-sensitive Indigos ran into when they began to incarnate in Earth's plane. Their sensitive systems were actually corrupted by foods that contained artificial additives that didn't resonate with their higher vibration. Many had reactions and health problems, such as attention deficit disorder (power failure)

> Organic diets hold a much higher vibration and thus are better suited to the transforming body and evolving psychic senses.

and hyperactivity (power surges), leading to misdiagnosis and overmedication. Their bodies simply could not hold the negative vibrations of all of the garbage going in. As a result, many Indigos developed serious medical conditions and mental disorders. The "old system" quite literally made them sick. The lucky ones who managed to avoid this grew into adults who initiated change and pioneered the way for the Crystals, Rainbows, and Star children so they would not fall prey to the same fate. Many Crystals and Rainbows have Indigo parents who know that organic diets hold a much higher vibration and thus are better suited to the transforming body and evolving psychic senses.

Managing Fear

Before Earth's shift into a new frequency, psychic abilities were viewed as a hoax or an anomaly at best, and an abnormality or curse at worst. Psychics usually had to put up with being thought of as unbalanced or a little "out there." The idea of psychic ability scares people because it has so many negative connotations, thanks to all the scammers, kooks, practitioners of the dark forces, and other misguided souls. The word *psychic* has its origins in the Greek word *psykhikos*, which means "of the soul or spirit." This seems to imply that your extrasensory, psychic side is connected somehow to your spiritual or energy nature. In other words, it is something wholesome and beneficial. Every now and then your logical mind may try to shut down your psychic side until your transformation is complete. Don't try to suppress your extrasensory senses, because you will likely block out useful information that could be of help to you or others (which, by the way, is the general purpose and highest good of being psychic in the first place).

Hopefully any concerns you may have about your awakened extrasensory senses have been somewhat ameliorated now that you know you are not losing your mind bur rather *expanding* it into the higher dimensions of consciousness. Even so, opening up to your psychic capabilities can be really scary for the rookie psychic because the feelings are so unfamiliar and strange. Initially, psychic hits and impressions can be a bit unsettling and even frightening, but don't dismiss them or tune them out because of this. I remember one particular day when I was *very* glad that I paid attention to the little voice inside my head: I was getting ready to go out when I heard an inner voice tell me to check the hot water tank in my utility closet. Now, I am not a handy person and I usually don't check these sorts of things unless there has already been a problem. The hot water tank was relatively new and I wasn't experiencing any problems with my water pressure, so I had no idea why I kept hearing the phrase *Check the water tank*. Sure enough, when I opened the utility closet there was a huge puddle of water under the tank. By listening to the psychic message in my head I managed to avoid a major problem that most likely would have left quite an expensive mess in my family room. Since then I have grown accustomed to my psychic sense of hearing and, moreover, actually *listening* to what I hear.

Psychic hearing manifests in different ways for different people. Before I receive a message I usually hear a high-pitched sound that alerts me that a message is incoming. In this way I've learned to tell the difference between self-talk and real information from the outside. I have spent many years as a practicing lightworker, and because I am open to my psychic senses I have experienced some amazing things. *Don't be afraid to tune in to your extrasensory channels*. You have a whole new dimension of consciousness to play around in and explore. The more you use your new abilities, the more adept you will become at discerning between the different kinds of energy. This is true knowing in its highest sense.

I have a funny story to relate about extrasensory smell that has a very practical application in this context. When you detect energy that comes from a higher vibration it will usually smell sweet or flowery. Low frequencies that are negative and possibly harmful will smell musty, "thick," and unpleasant. A few years ago a psychic I knew was working along with a few other psychics trying to help the police find a missing person. Most of the psychics in the group agreed that the person they were looking for was purposefully hiding and would turn up in a week or so. However, one of the psychics strongly disagreed and said that she *definitely* smelled death. As a matter of fact, she said with great anxiety that the odor was getting closer and stronger by the minute. Well, the odor was most definitely getting stronger: It just so happened that she had inadvertently

Don't be afraid to tune in to your extrasensory channels.

stepped in something unpleasant and it was on the bottom of her shoe. The rule of thumb is to always check the bottom of your shoes first to make sure there isn't a more...well, prosaic explanation for your impressions! Regardless, it is always a good practice to repeat an affirmation that only messages for your highest good are allowed to tune in to your frequency.

If you receive an impression of something that is negative or upsetting—or something that you would rather not see at all—send out transmuting energy toward the premonition and obliterate it from your mind's eye. This is similar to changing the channel when you don't want to watch something on TV. Just because you are suddenly psychic doesn't mean that you can't shut down your psychic portals if you find that you are getting bombarded with too many impressions. Just as you close your eyes when you go to sleep, you can also willingly put your extrasensory senses into a kind of sleep mode to avoid psychic burnout. The main thing is to always use your new awakened senses responsibly; no matter how tempting it is, *do not* use your enhanced sensory powers to infringe upon the will, rights, or space of another person. The energy you put out, whether negative or positive, always returns to its source, so always keep it positive.

> You can willingly put your extrasensory senses into a kind of sleep mode to avoid psychic burnout.

Some Practical Applications
Remote Viewing

Eventually you may be able to use your psychic senses for remote viewing. Remote viewing is a form of clairvoyance originally developed as a tool for military and intelligence operations. Yes, even the typically left-brained military realized the value of and potential in extrasensory sensing. Remote viewing often involves "zoning in" to

> Always use your new awakened senses responsibly.

look at a specific building, location, or object (the "target") in order to gain knowledge that would otherwise be impossible to obtain. Remote viewing also entails picking up scents, hearing conversations through clairaudience, and even drawing pictures of what is seen. Your transformation gives you access to the kind of sight and insight that was once the sole provenance of government-trained professionals. This is also where learning to protect your psychic privacy comes into play. Without this, you run the risk of becoming a paranormal TV show for the curious or, worse, the sinister.

Psychometry and Healing

Now that you are evolved and awakened to your provocative psychic senses, holding or touching an object will enable you to immediately discover a great deal of information about it—where it's been, with whom it came into contact, and what energetic impressions were left behind on it. *Psychometry*, or psychic touch, allows you to "read" these impressions and make certain deductions. When this ability is lined up with the frequency of love from the Heart chakra, it also gives you the ability to heal through massage or the laying on of hands. By way of an example, I once had a terrible headache. I focused my attention on my hands for a few minutes and charged them with a greenish hue (green exerts a soothing influence on both mind and body). After I felt that I had infused enough healing energy into my hands, I placed them on each side of my head and allowed the green light to go in and relax the tension. Somehow I knew to move my hands back and forth, which decreased the pain even more. I could feel the energy move through my fingers and into my head, exploding and radiating beautiful green healing energy. Within four or five minutes my headache was completely gone. I had successfully used this particular version of psychometry, healing touch, to transmute

> When this ability is lined up with the frequency of love from the Heart chakra, it gives you the ability to heal through massage or the laying on of hands.

the frequency of pain to a neutral state. Every form of matter, when broken down to the smallest particle, changes into waves, which are nothing but a form of energy—which we now have the ability to manipulate and alter at will. What a wonderful way to use one's gifts!

Communicating Telepathically

In order to successfully prepare yourself for telepathic communication, it is important to clear your mind, center yourself by grounding all excess energy, and concentrate on being in the moment. To send a telepathic message you will need two participants: a receiver and a sender. Some people are better receivers, while others are better at sending messages. Close friends and family members are usually the easiest to reach at first because you already have a familiar resonance with one another. Like all your gifts, telepathy should never be used for manipulation or coercion. Thought-forms should always come from a higher consciousness because lower vibrations only ascend so far and usually produce undesirable results. You don't make crank phone calls, do you? So don't send out crank telepathic messages either, because manifestation of intention is instantaneous and impossible to recall. Be mindful of your thoughts, because they can be picked up by others within your frequency band.

Seeing Ghosts

Perhaps the most sensational (and often disquieting) aspect of being *Homo sentient* is the ability to see spirits. The shift into a higher consciousness now opens up a whole new world of energy to us, including spirit energy. Some common sightings include ghosts, trapped energy, spirits, and even interdimensional beings from other galactic communities. The more adept you become at using your clairaudience, the more easily you will be able to tune in to the frequencies of the departed. This will happen only when they wish to communicate with you, so don't think that you aren't clairaudient if you can't reach a loved one who has passed over. Don't allow doubt a foothold, because doubt blocks your ability to tune in to the spiritual realms. You may very well make contact with a guide from the higher dimensions who has come to assist you, but always remember to say a prayer or affirmation of protection to ensure that only positive spirits appear. Although guides themselves are usually positive entities, anyone opening up psychical-ly may be subject to negative energies as well. Carl Jung had several spirit guides (Philemon being the most notable) who contacted him when he was 3 years old and ended up tutoring him most of his life.

> Doubt blocks your ability to tune in to the spiritual realms.

Many children have "make believe" or invisible friends when they are very young. It is very likely that these "friends" are actually guides or protector spirits.

When your guides come forward, be prepared to accept whatever guidance they offer—again, as long as they are positive entities. Here is the rule for dealing with spirit guides: They are not allowed to interfere with your free will; they can only advise. If a spirit tries to get you to do something that you would rather not do or something that runs counter to your moral code, that is probably your first clue that you are deal-ing with a negative entity. Be wary of tricksters. If you do not want to see spirits, apparitions, or thought-forms (and not everyone does), you have the ability to simply tune them out. It's similar to changing the dial from FM to AM: Yes, the FM radio frequencies are still out there, but you won't be able to tune in and listen unless you change bandwidths. By keeping your own frequency high and using the proper precautions mentioned in this chapter, you limit the risk of becoming a host for nega-tive entities.

When you first tune in to spirit energy you may only see orbs of light. You will be able to sense if the orbs are good or bad usually by their color, speed, and frequency. You will know if they are light or dense by the vibrations you feel in their presence. Sometimes an orb will morph into an actual form. If you sense that the intentions of the manifested spirit are bad, ask it to leave; then, visualize a shield around yourself to protect your own aura from any unwanted attachments.

Telekinesis

Telekinesis involves manipulating the energy in matter so that it bends or moves. Everything is made of the same thing (energy); therefore, manipulating energy (and hence matter) is essentially just a form of communicating with it. This may seem more like a party trick than a useful ability, but when you get into creative visualization and manifesting you will see how important this ability really is. An easy way to familiarize yourself with how energy feels when it moves is to make psi balls. Psi balls are basically balls of energy that you form in your hands and then send outward to accomplish a task. To make a psi ball, hold your hands apart as if you were holding a soccer ball and focus on feeling the energy build between the palms of your hands. Move your hands around to "form" a ball shape in the air; you will begin to feel heat, tingly sensations, and even itching on your palms as you manipulate the energy. Once you have successfully shaped the energy, visually inject a color into the ball and then release it by gently tossing it toward a solid object. Watch it burst apart as it disseminates the energy around its desired target. Be especially mindful when choosing a color for your psi ball, as each color has its own energy. If you want to send someone a ball of healing energy, use green. Be careful with the color red because it can translate as anger if you're ungrounded. Following is a list of some colors you can experiment with.

> Everything is made of the same thing (energy); therefore, manipulating energy (and hence matter) is essentially just a form of communicating with it.

* ❀ **Cool colors (calming):** blue, green, turquoise, and silver.
* ❀ **Warm colors (exciting):** red, pink, yellow, gold, and orange.
* ❀ **Mixed colors (healing):** purple, lavender, green, and turquoise/teal.
* ❀ **Neutral colors (unifying):** brown, beige, ivory, gray, black, and white.

I'll state it once again for emphasis: Always use your new "toys" respectfully and responsibly. Energy put out will always return to source. Don't make psi balls filled with negative intentions and aim them at someone unless you plan on taking that same energy back. I like to use psi balls to energize

> Always use your new "toys" respectfully and responsibly.

tasks, to keep my energy moving and get tasks done more efficiently. I've found that psi balls filled with bright orange or yellow stimulate my creativity and encourage creative manifestation.

Teleportation (It's Not Just for Trekkies Anymore)

Did you know that your transformation also opens up a whole new way for you to travel? The military has been researching teleportation (the process of moving matter from one location to another instantaneously) for years. You know that if the government is trying to harness an extrasensory capability, there must be something to it! Here is a little background information on teleportation that will hopefully remove some of the mystery and sci-fi aspect. Great mystics and saints have actually been able to teleport, and several Christian saints and monks are said to have exhibited bilocation (being in two places at once). In 1774, St. Alphonsus Liguori went into a trance while preparing for Mass. When he came out of the trance he said that he had visited the bedside of the dying Pope Clement XIV. Those attending to the ailing Pope confirmed that St. Alphonsus Liquori has indeed been there in the room, even though he lived far

> One day you may be able to simply pass through solid matter and even shift from one location to another instantaneously.

away and had never left his original location. This is not just for saints and mystics, however; you are now privy to this mystery if you open up to it. One day you may be able to simply pass through solid matter and even shift from one location to another instantaneously. As you can see, you will eventually be blessed with powers that most people today would describe as miraculous or magical. Just remember that everyone hones their extrasensory abilities differently, and you may find that some psychic abilities resonate better with your own personal frequency than others. Staying grounded and protected is vital if you are to have positive experiences. And of course you will also need to know what to filter out so you don't become overwhelmed functioning in those higher frequencies.

Learning to live in this new world of frequency and energy really forces you to embrace a whole new set of priorities. Eventually you will get over your growing pains and be able to maneuver decisively and confidently through or around any obstacle or threat. And remember that there are always healers, lightworkers, consultants, and guides (physical and spiritual) available to help you along the way. This is what we will turn our attention to next.

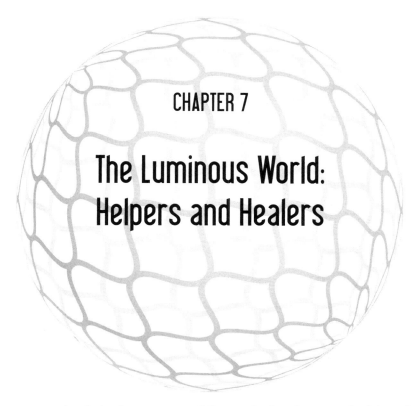

CHAPTER 7

The Luminous World: Helpers and Healers

The greatest mistake in the treatment of diseases is that there are physicians for the body and physicians for the soul, although the two cannot be separated.

—Plato

The first few chapters of this book showed you how your recalibrated chakras are adjusting to the new wave of consciousness, thereby allowing for the opening up and advancement of your psychic senses. Your transformation also gives you the opportunity to transmute any negative attachments from your aura to bring about a higher vibration, which itself leads to better health. At times these evolutionary changes can short-circuit your energy because they involve getting used to functioning from a higher level of vibration. Traditional doctors are (sometimes) good for the body, but energy imbalances and psychic malfunctions are best left to practitioners who are familiar with different healing modalities and

> Your transformation gives you the opportunity to transmute any negative attachments from your aura to bring about a higher vibration, which itself leads to better health.

integrated medicine so you can be healed on all levels—body, mind, and spirit. Addressing only the physical problem leaves you vulnerable to relapse because the vibration that caused the illness may still be active in the form of a vibration or thought-form. Even just saying the name of an illness or condition can put you at a higher risk of co-creating a relapse. Remember that sound is a powerful creative frequency that, when coupled with your emotional energy and beliefs, can manifest into a real experience. Living in victim consciousness eventually breeds discomfort and even illness. Fortunately, once you reach a state of higher awareness you'll have a much better understanding of how your thoughts affect your well-being. Noted psychiatrist and spiritual teacher Dr. David R. Hawkins has often stated that unconscious guilt, self-perpetuating beliefs, and suppressed emotions are behind virtually all health problems. He is correct. So where do you go when your spiritual body is feeling...well, off?

During your transformation and evolution, guides, teachers, and healers will show up periodically as you venture into the dimensions of higher consciousness. Included in this group are the lightworkers, the souls who are here to provide basic information about your transformation and offer holistic treatments and remedies for your newly awakened self. Other healers include the Crystal, Indigo, Rainbow, and Star children. If you have ever had a creative, sensitive, avant-garde friend, he or she was most likely an adult Indigo, one of the group that is leading the revolution of authentic living and helping pave the way for the rebirth of the world. Indigos are the revolutionaries who are tearing down all the false belief systems to make space for a newly defined reality that shuns materialism. Likewise, if you've ever had a psychic friend who was more quiet and empathic, he or she was most likely an adult Crystal, one of the group that is here to help us transition into a kinder, gentler society so we can all be part of a more refined collective consciousness.

Some of the teachers and guides you will meet are called "Specials." These are people who are natural receptors of messages from future/parallel lives. They have had their frequencies adjusted through telepathic signaling from helpful, nonhuman entities, such as spirits, who coexist with us in a parallel state—a dimension or vibrational medium that is normally invisible to us. In addition to spirit influence, benevolent extraterrestrials from other star systems often choose Specials as their emissaries to help humanity evolve. They do this through the use of BWE (Brain Wave Entrainment, possibly through implanted devices) and repeated exposure to symbols, numerical patterns, and crop circles. Like the Crystals, Specials possesses a gentleness and a very calm demeanor. Specials who have never had access to their psychic nature often find that after a series of unusual synchronistic events, lucid dreams, OBEs, or possibly even an abduction experience, they suddenly have an epiphany of enlightenment. Their brain is now an open doorway to infinite intelligence, while their heart does the actual communicating through love and empathy. They are here to form a bridge to our guides and galactic neighbors as we go through the empowering shift of consciousness. Many Specials are innovative thinkers in the fields of technology, science, and medicine. As you evolve, you, too, will realize that it is possible to have your heart and your brain waves recoded by certain frequencies that influence and elevate consciousness. The Rainbow and Star children who showed up after the Indigos and Crystals are very sensitive to frequency waves and tend to communicate via telepathy, which is also the way that higher beings and aliens communicate. These two groups are here specifically to help recalibrate the frequency of Earth and set the tone for advanced, extrasensory living.

Lightworkers who have been around since the early stages of the energy shift are old souls who have retained the knowledge of energy-healing that was initially programmed into our DNA many life incarnations

> It is possible to have your heart and your brain waves recoded by certain frequencies that influence and elevate consciousness.

ago. These lightworkers are like emergency room doctors who are ready to rush in and triage a patient until he or she is stabilized enough for treatment. They are the shamans and mystics who have done this work many times over throughout many lives. For this reason they often possess uncanny abilities when it comes to helping and healing those who are having difficulty evolving. Some of these teachers and guides go all the way back to the days of Atlantis and have incarnated throughout the ages to help foster humanity's evolution to enlightenment.

> Lightworkers are here to help you let go of old structures and beliefs and move into the flow of the fifth dimension.

Lightworkers are here to help you let go of old structures and beliefs and move into the flow of the fifth dimension. Because events will be unfolding rapidly, you will need to be flexible and open to changes so you don't delay or halt your evolution. The more tightly you hold on to old beliefs and structures that don't serve your highest good, the more anxiety and stress you will create for yourself. Shifting out of drama and into a freer-flowing mode of living isn't always easy, because there is usually a great deal of work to be done in releasing limited and limiting thought patterns. Staying positive throughout all of these changes won't always be easy, either, because the antiquated emotion of fear will sometimes raise its ugly head. If this is something you experience, you may need the help of a lightworker to help you rebirth yourself through all of these changes. Following is a list of some of the most proficient and proactive practitioners and healing methods that will keep you tuned up and tuned in as you adjust to your new consciousness.

Quantum Healing and Vibrational Medicine

The basic premise of quantum healing is that the mind can heal the body. In quantum healing, *all* layers of your being are treated—the physical body, the mind, and the spirit—to help you conquer physical ailments. This process involves touch healing, energy healing, and spiritual healing techniques to energize your *chi*, or life force. Our physical body is a complex system made up of cells that register and resonate with everything we experience. Our aura holds the frequencies from our beliefs, emotions, and experiences as a sort of library; when we feel sad, angry, upset, or distressed, the messages are directly relayed to every cell in our body. When we fall ill, our body is simply registering an energy blockage within the aura and manifesting it on the physical level. Quantum healing has actually been around for many thousands of years. Eastern medicine, Indian/Vedic healing techniques, and even religious faith healing are all forms of this method. All are based upon a deep knowledge that the mind has a most powerful impact upon the body.

A quantum healing session with an alternative medical professional usually starts with an energy assessment. The practitioner may lightly touch your body or place his or her hands just above the area of pain, illness, or injury. You will be asked to relax and focus on your breathing in order to achieve a meditative state so your mind can begin the healing process. You may feel sensations of heat, cold, or tingling as the practitioner manipulates the energy blockage(s) to accelerate healing. After a session it is not uncommon to feel incredibly energized. Pain and illness can be greatly relieved. Keep in mind that *you* are actually the healer in the sense that you enable the healing work to happen; the practitioner is merely the facilitator. Many chiropractors, physical therapists, acupuncturists, and osteopaths are now beginning to incorporate quantum healing methods into their practices. Quantum healing also amplifies the effects of Reiki because it works with our personal energy from within, whereas Reiki works with the universal life force without. When the two are integrated, healing can be augmented.

The mind can heal the body.

My Reiki Master, Mary P. O'Donnell, told me about her teacher and mentor, Hannelore Christensen, an amazing healer, shaman, and Reiki Master. When I first met Hannelore I could immediately sense the healing energy emanating from her aura. Hannelore is well versed in different healing modalities, herbs, bodywork, Reiki, and energy-clearing methods that are necessary for anyone who needs help shifting into the empowering transformation. She comes from a long line of heal-ers, which she cites as the source of her abilities. Her healing gifts are encoded into her DNA, and there is no doubt that she has done this work previously in other lifetimes. Hannelore has successfully helped people heal both physically and emotionally by treating them with en-ergy medicine and natural, holistic remedies. According to Hannelore, many of our problems originate in our reluctance to let go and detach from the buildup of emotional and material attachments. We attach our-selves to things that give us the illusion of abundance but that, in reality, bring about stress, the precursor to illness. This over-attachment to the material world and the stress that goes with it will build up energy walls, and these walls eventually turn into a box, trapping you in false beliefs. Sometimes these walls are thin and transparent, and at other times they can be extremely dense and opaque—especially those that come from lifetimes of repeated negative patterns of behavior. In order for you to be in full alignment with the higher frequency that supports your evolution and transformation, this trapped energy needs to be cleared out.

As a gifted lightworker, Hannelore helps people get rid of limiting blocks that cause anxiety and can eventually bring about illness. Her objective in healing is to get someone's energy moving again; this may entail physical exercises, reflexology, and/or massage sessions (to release embedded memories still held within the muscles). Sometimes ceremo-nies and herb packs are recommended in addition to the massage and bodywork. As she explains, every healing is different and depends en-tirely on the person and his or her individual needs. One of her diagnostic methods involves holding on to the patient's arm to feel the flow of the energy going through his or her body. In this way she can sense where there may be blockages stifling the per-son's shift into higher conscious-ness. I once asked her if she works with a specific guide as part of her work, and she assured me that she never rules anyone out.

We attach ourselves to things that give us the illusion of abundance but that, in reality, bring about stress, the precursor to illness.

The right person usually steps forward to give her the information she needs to proceed with a healing. Her guides have included the archangels, Buddha, the spirits of Native Americans—basically anyone on the other side of the veil who was able to be of assistance.

The newly ascending body is extremely sensitive to energy and frequency changes. What may seem like outdated healing methods are actually the most effective ways to treat people who are opening up to their true nature. Hannelore follows *mitakuye oyasin*, a Lakota Sioux word meaning "all my relations" or "we are all related." This refers to the fact that everything—nature, the heavens, each other, even the creative force itself—is a part of one consciousness. What is not in mitakuye oyasin will eventually fall away because it will not be needed in the state of higher consciousness. She also stresses the fact that energy-clearing must be performed at all levels in order to get everything back into balance. Addressing the body, mind, and spirit as one definitely helps, but the patient's environment also needs to be cleared of any emotional residue that is contributing to the "heavy" atmosphere. Energy has a tendency to linger, especially in corners, so it is imperative to clear out the patient's space.

My cousin Dottie once called upon Hannelore and Mary when she was experiencing an energy disturbance inside her home. Dottie had always felt a strange presence in the house, especially in one particular room. The presence was so strong that two cleaning ladies ended up quitting because of the weird goings-on. The room in question contained several dolls that, according to one of the cleaning women, moved and even talked. The stress from the heavy presence in Dottie's home was causing her to feel anxious and unnerved. Hannelore and Mary showed up at Dottie's home and proceeded to do a space clearing both inside and outside the building. Dottie told me that they even cleared out her personal energy to make sure that there weren't any energy attachments that would continue to drain her and make her feel uneasy. They smudged the house with sage, and performed a ceremony of drumming and rattling to help move the energy along its way.

It turns out that the house had been built on a Native American burial ground; as you can imagine, the land itself held a great deal of energy, both positive and negative. When Hannelore and Mary discovered wild herbs and plants behind the house that the tribe used to grow, this was confirmation to them that the land had once been a well-tended sacred space. The energy surrounding and emanating from this particular tribe was crossing over into the current reality. Hannelore and Mary knew they had to clear the energy so that Dottie's reality would no longer pick up any energetic residue from the ceremonial site. Every now and then Dottie still feels that same energy make its presence known, but she now knows to ask it to recede and go back to its own plane of existence.

> Uniting with the world of energy around you helps you realize that there is a lot more to life than just the physical world.

As you can see, uniting with the world of energy around you helps you realize that there is a lot more to life than just the physical world. When you experience glitches in your system you should know where to go for assistance. A skilled energy-worker such as Hannelore Christensen is a must for your contact list of whom to call when you are in need of energy-grounding, clearing, healing, and/or transmutation.

Integrated Medicine

Integrated medicine brings together the most current scientific advances with ancient healing modalities. This "best of both worlds" approach gives you access to the most effective ways to preserve your physical, mental, *and* psychic health. Every illness has behind it an emotion that holds a vibration that can then be transmuted via healing. Don't forget that you now have self-healing abilities as one of the benefits of your evolution. The more familiar you become with the world of energy, the more you will begin to realize that illnesses usually have a nonphysical origin. When illness manifests on the physical level, you'll know that it wasn't addressed or stopped in the emotional and mental levels where it first originated.

Dr. Royal R. Rife, a 20th-century American inventor and scientist, developed a machine that applies currents of specific frequencies to the body to cure a wide range of diseases. It works by using a variable frequency, pulsed radio transmitter to produce resonance within the cells of the physical body. He noted that every disease has a specific frequency, and that certain frequencies can prevent the development of disease or obliterate an existing pathology. Substances with higher frequencies will destroy diseases of a lower frequency. Not surprisingly, Dr. Rife's findings were discredited by the traditional medical community. He felt that this was part of a powerful conspiracy of people who knew there was more money in keeping people sick than in curing them of their illnesses. Of course, this runs contrary to the original version of the Hippocratic Oath, which states in part, "I will follow that system of regimen which, according to my ability and judgment, I consider for the benefit of my patients, and abstain from whatever is deleterious and mischievous. I will give *no deadly medicine to any one if asked, nor suggest any such counsel*" (emphasis mine).

When illness manifests on the physical level, you'll know that it wasn't addressed or stopped in the emotional and mental levels where it first originated.

Fortunately, we are now enlightened enough to realize that we must balance our energy first, by altering our thoughts, eating better-quality food, and keeping our environment as free from stress as possible. Some of the more common diseases, such as cancer, contain the frequency of the emotion of resentment, which, literally and figuratively, eats away the self. As alternatives to chemotherapy and radiation treatments, healing modalities that include positive mantras, adjusted diets, Reiki, and prayer have successfully put cancer patients into remission because they address the

The vibrations of disease can be shifted into neutral or positive frequencies once the body, mind, and spirit are aligned during a healing.

cause before the cure. The vibrations of disease can be shifted into neutral or positive frequencies once the body, mind, and spirit are aligned during a healing.

Enumerating all of the amazing healthcare options available to treat your newly evolved self isn't possible here because there are myriad ways to change the frequency of illness. I will list some of the more popular treatments and healing modalities that will keep you physically, mentally, and psychically fit, and that will resonate with your transformation.

Aromatherapy

Aromatherapy is the use of aromatic essential oils for psychological, physical, and extrasensory well-being. This healing art has its roots in antiquity. Every scent has a vibration that helps the body recalibrate its energy and recover from a stressful situation. In aromatherapy, scents are specially blended for the individual by a trained aromatherapist, and either inhaled by the patient through a diffuser or directly massaged into the skin. This practice takes into account the fact that your physical body will resonate at certain frequencies depending on the state of your health. A healthy body typically has a range of 62–78 MHz, with disease beginning at 58 MHz. If the frequency drops to 58 MHz or below, cold and flu symptoms appear; at 55 MHz certain chronic diseases and conditions appear; at 52 MHz chronic fatigue syndrome appears; and at 42 MHz, cancer is a real possibility. Death occurs at 25 MHz. Everything, from the food you eat to the thoughts you think, has a direct effect on your physical body, which, as you now know, is a direct manifestation of your spiritual self.

Following is a list of some of your most vital body organs along with their associated ranges of frequencies. After your evolutionary shift, these rates can increase by at least 10 percent—not surprising, really, because you will be holding more light.

Body Organ	Frequency in Megahertz
Ascending Colon	50–60 MHz
Descending Colon	58–63 MHz
Heart	67–70 MHz
Liver	55–60 MHz
Lungs	58–65 MHz
Pancreas	60–80 MHz
Stomach	58–65 MHz
Thymus	65–68 MHz
Thyroid and Parathyroid	62–68 MHz

Studies have shown that the frequencies from essential oils can create an environment in which disease, bacteria, viruses, and mold cannot survive. These oils also keep the chakras spinning at the right vibrations. You can actually raise your overall frequency by using the proper essential oil or oil blend.

Your body is very sensitive to frequencies that interact with its own vibration. Having an argument with someone can lower your frequency; so can eating the wrong foods. Your body is so sensitive that even holding a cup of coffee—or a negative thought—can have an adverse effect on your body's vibes. It is a proven fact that when you inhale essential oils, your bodily frequency can return to normal within 21 seconds. Research shows that essential oils have the highest

> The frequencies from essential oils can create an environment in which disease, bacteria, viruses, and mold cannot survive.

frequencies of any known natural substance. They start at 52 MHz and go as high as 320 MHz (pure rose oil). The frequencies of essential oils have the ability to help restore and maintain optimal health, and create an environment in which stress (the precursor to disease) can't prevail. They can also raise your frequency high enough to enable you to tap into the spirit realms.

As you will recall from previous chapters, your chakra centers handle and process your body's electromagnetic energy. They also serve as vortices for the flow of energy from the physical to the subtle bodies (emotional, mental, and etheric). Certain essential oils support this unique physio-psychic system, especially during and after your transformation. Following is a list of your chakras and the essential oils recommended for each, along with a troubleshooting guide. Keep in mind that a medical professional should be consulted before you attempt to self-treat any problem or condition.

Root chakra: The best essential oils for your Root chakra include peppermint, cedar wood, clove, patchouli, ginger, vetiver, frankincense, myrrh, cardamom, laurel, and sandalwood. The body parts governed by the root chakra are the lymph system, the skeletal system, the digestive system, and the lower extremities. If this chakra is blocked, you will feel fearful, anxious, insecure, and frustrated. Physical indicators such as obesity, anorexia nervosa, and knee troubles can occur. If you experience any of these conditions in those areas of your body, investigate the areas in life where you don't feel grounded. Your psychic sense of smell, clairscent, can be fine-tuned by using these scents.

> Your chakra centers handle and process your body's electromagnetic energy.

Sacral chakra: Essential oils for your Sacral chakra include ylang-ylang, myrrh, coriander, rose, geranium, jasmine, cinnamon, tangerine, pine cypress, rose geranium, and patchouli. The main body parts governed by this chakra are the reproductive system, sexual organs, bladder, kidneys, and middle spine. If this chakra is blocked, you may feel emotionally explosive, become manipulative, and become obsessed with thoughts of sex. Physical problems show up as kidney weakness, a stiff lower back, constipation, and muscle spasms. Water retention is associated with this chakra, particularly if the emotions are greatly repressed or not expressed in the most effective way. Clairgustation, or psychic taste, can be honed by using these recommended essential oils.

Solar Plexus chakra: The Solar Plexus chakra is best maintained by using lemon, ginger, carrot, juniper, rosemary, oregano, vetiver, peppermint, citronella, lemongrass, cedar wood, marjoram, cinnamon bark, cardamom, and valerian oils. This chakra center governs the stomach, liver, gall bladder, pancreas, and small intestine. When this chakra is out of balance you will lack confidence, act confused, worry about what others think, and get depressed. You will also have difficulty concentrating, an inability to make decisions or judge a situation accurately, and trouble taking action or getting things done. This chakra is where boundary issues come into play. Physical problems include digestive difficulties, liver problems, diabetes, and food allergies. Your psychic sense of precognition, your "gut" feeling, is best maintained with these oils.

Heart chakra: This chakra encompasses the heart, lungs, circulatory system, shoulders, and upper back, and is best maintained by oils such as melissa, frankincense, bergamot, carrot, lavender, marjoram, sandalwood, hyssop, laurel, spikenard, camphor, and cinnamon bark. When this chakra is out of balance you may feel pity, paranoia, jealousy, anger, and dependence on someone else for your happiness. Physical problems include heart attack, high blood pressure, insomnia, and difficulty breathing. Psychometry and psychic healing touch are kept in optimum working condition by using the recommended essential oils for this chakra center.

Throat chakra: The best essential oils for your Throat chakra are chamomile, catnip, cypress, spruce, carrot seed, lavender, spearmint, frankincense, and geranium. The body parts associated with the fifth chakra are throat, neck, teeth, ears, and thyroid gland. When this chakra center isn't in tune, addictions, the need to criticize, habitual lying, lack of authority, and indecisiveness can present themselves. Physical problems and imbalances will show up as sore throats, mouth ulcers, swollen glands, thyroid dysfunctions, laryngitis, voice problems, and gum or tooth problems. Clairaudience, your ability to hear in a paranormal manner, can be maintained and honed by using the oils mentioned.

Third Eye chakra: The clairvoyant abilities of this chakra are best served by essential oils of cedar, spruce, rosemary, oregano, thyme, linden, and clary sage. This chakra is vital to your transformation and evolution into higher consciousness. It relates to the brain, neurological system, eyes, ears, nose, and pituitary and pineal glands. Imbalances in this chakra show up as a fear of truth, bad judgment, compromised emotional intelligence, and a distorted concept of reality filled with confusion. Physical problems manifest as tension headaches, migraines, visual defects, near-sightedness/far-sightedness, glaucoma, cataracts, and sinus problems. Keep your psychic abilities of telepathy, astral travel, connecting into parallel lives, and clairvoyance/psychic sight in balance by tuning your frequency to the aromas of the oils mentioned here.

Crown chakra: This chakra bridges the gap between body and spirit. The best essential oils include cistus, myrrh, angelica, lavender, rose, basil, rosemary, and ravensara. This chakra is associated with the top of the head, the brain, and the entire nervous system. When it is unbalanced there is frustration, joylessness, mental illness, senility, and destructive feelings. Physical problems can include severe migraine headaches and depression. Conversely, when this chakra is balanced, we have access to both the unconscious and the subconscious. The master extrasensory sense associated with the Crown chakra is Divine knowing; the recommended essential oils will help keep you plugged in to the Source of the universe.

Eighth chakra: This energy center will be activated during your evolutionary shift. It sits about an arm's length above the Crown chakra. The essential oils for this chakra are neroli and, of course, rose, which has the highest frequency. This chakra, the energy center of Divine love, spiritual compassion, and spiritual selflessness, connects to your aura and the Akashic Record, the master recording of all of your incarnations. Because this chakra is so closely connected to the Divine it usually does not contain any shadow emotions or imbalances; if the other chakras aren't in balance it will not open up. When this chakra is balanced we reach beyond the material and psychic planes and into the full-blown spiritual dimensions, which are supported by the recommended oils for this chakra.

"Buddha Belly" chakra: This new chakra is kept at the right frequency by using pure essential oils such as ylang-ylang, lavender, geranium, sandalwood, and blue tansy. This chakra relates to the diaphragm and lungs. When it is unbalanced, emotional drama is usually the result. Physical conditions include breathing problems, asthma, and weight gain carried around the midsection (stress weight). Using the essential oils listed here will help to keep this chakra clear and balanced, which in turn will help you process emotional energy and avoid drama.

Thymus chakra: This newly formed chakra responds best to oils of myrrh, orange, and petitgrain. This chakra relates to the thymus gland and the immune system, and contains the entire pattern for your DNA as well as your cellular memory from all life incarnations. When this chakra is weak, blocked, or imbalanced, enmeshment, over-protectiveness, greed, and anger may result. The physical symptoms of an unbalanced Thymus chakra are autoimmune conditions such as rheumatoid arthritis. This chakra helps you regulate the intentions behind your thoughts so you can achieve the best results when using your newly opened psychic sensory system.

Aromatherapy is as much an art as it is a science. The aroma from essential oils can be useful for healings, for beautifying, and for inducing the necessary frequencies to rev up your psychic senses. Plus, they are just plain fun to use!

Crystal Healing

"Getting stoned," if you'll pardon the pun, may be another path to optimum health. Today's holistic health practitioners understand that certain stones can ease physical, mental, and spiritual discomfort. In fact, the use of crystals for healing has gone mainstream. You already know that your body has a certain energy vibration, and that each organ of the body also has its own distinct frequency. When we take an energy hit from a stressful situation or some other negative facilitator of low voltage, our subtle energy body takes the first blow. If we fail to correct any disturbances, the results are usually mirrored as physical discomfort. Because you are becoming more crystal-based and less carbon-based, crystal therapy is a good choice for encouraging and maintaining health. Crystals can be worn as jewelry, carried in pouches, placed on the body, and even added to massage oils and lotions. You can even make drinkable crystal elixirs. Now there are all kinds of health benefits to having your drink "on the rocks."

> Your body has a certain energy vibration, and each organ of the body also has its own distinct frequency.

Healthcare professionals who use crystals for healing are often very sought after, especially by people who are tired of being poisoned by medications that mask symptoms but fail to get at the root cause. Some crystals and stones even help you avoid the impact of stress-related disease in the first place by acting as a barrier against illness—take, for example, hematite, which is known to deflect negative energy. Crystals can receive and hold thought-forms, which means you can program them for specific healings. Following is a list of some of the more popular healing stones and crystals and how they can help you through your transformation into higher consciousness. As with any energy-sensitive substance, some stones may not be a good fit for you if they carry the wrong frequency. Always consult an expert prior to using crystal medicine.

Amethyst has long been called the sobriety stone. It is said to assist with healing alcoholism and addictions of all kinds. It also helps with headaches and, when placed near the Brow chakra, is effective in opening up a person psychically.

Aquamarine is the stone of courage. It has tranquilizing properties. It will quiet the mind and reduce stress. This stone also helps relieve water retention, especially as your body adjusts to the new, higher frequencies of transformation. Place it on the Throat chakra to heal a sore throat.

Black tourmaline is excellent for grounding excess energy. It is often used as an aura cleanser, and is a great stone to ward off psychic attack. Black tourmaline has also been used to deflect radiation energy from TVs and computer monitors. It is good for strengthening the immune system, and is helpful in heart disease, arthritis, and gout. This stone relates to the Root chakra.

Bloodstone helps one accept change and overcome the anxiety, depression, and melancholia that is often associated with energy shift. This stone helps cure psychosomatic illnesses, purifies the blood, and detoxifies organs (especially the liver, where we tend to hold anger).

Citrine is known to enhance mental clarity, confidence, and willpower. Citrine is purported to alleviate depression and self-doubt and diminish irrational mood swings, which may be more prevalent during your transformation. Citrine is associated with the Solar Plexus chakra and aids in manifesting prosperity.

Clear quartz is a power stone that harmonizes and balances. It enhances energy and thoughts, and purifies the spiritual, mental, and physical. It is used to perform diagnostic healing and unblock specific areas or organs that are unable to transmit or receive energy. Clear quartz is primarily associated with the Crown chakra, but it works equally well on all the other chakras. Clear quartz is also considered to be the only crystal that can clear other crystals. Placing your other crystals on top of quartz will cleanse them of any negativity. This stone was the master crystal of Atlantis.

Emerald is the recommended stone for heart and lung health, swollen lymph nodes, blood problems, the thymus, the pancreas (for blood sugar rebalance), labor and delivery, and eyesight. Excellent for general healing, it has been considered a blood detoxifier and poison antidote since ancient times. It helps strengthen the backbone and alleviates problems associated with diabetes. The emerald is most effective now that we are evolving. This stone supports the expanding Heart chakra and enables conscious breathing.

Garnet regenerates the body and stimulates metabolism. It treats disorders of the spine and spinal fluid, bone, and cellular structure and composition; purifies the heart, lungs, and blood; and regenerates DNA. Garnet also boosts the immune system and energy levels. It is highly recommended now that our DNA is changing due to our transformation to higher consciousness.

Lapis lazuli enhances the interconnectedness of the higher bodies with the physical body. Lapis primarily affects the throat areas; it aids the speech center and the ability to communicate freely. Lapis stimulates the thyroid and harmonizes its functions as well as that of the kidneys, helping with elimination of toxins and reducing high blood pressure. Lapis lazuli has a profound effect on female hormonal balance. It usually lengthens the menstrual cycle by two days. In menopausal women it can induce the return of the regular menstrual cycle. Lapis has proven itself as a tool for weight loss by reducing the fat levels in the blood and tissues. It also aids in tuning your ability for clairaudience and in overcoming depression. Lapis lazuli should always be worn above the diaphragm, as close to the Throat chakra as possible.

Lepidolite is a stone with an extremely high vibration. It works on the brain's pain centers, helping to alleviate drug addiction and bipolar disorder, and stabilize mood swings. Lepidolite is good for reducing stress, depression, despondency, obsessive thinking, and any confusion brought about by the evolutionary shift. Lepidolite activates the Throat, Heart, Brow, and Crown chakras, bringing cosmic awareness and aiding deep meditation by clearing unwanted energetic debris from the mind.

Lithium quartz is an extremely high-energy healing and balancing stone. An incredibly versatile stone, it sends, receives, and stores energy. Lithium quartz is balancing and calming, and is used in crystal healing as a natural antidepressant. It is said to relieve stress, anxiety, and tension, bringing relaxation and peace. It is also used to help relieve muscular tension and repetitive motion injuries. Lithium quartz both activates and balances all of the chakras, which is crucial during our evolution.

Peridot helps bring energy from the aura into the physical body. It aids in understanding and accepting change, and provides a protective shield around the body. It is used in treating emotional states such as anger or jealousy. It is associated with stress reduction, relaxation, comfort, and intuition, and is especially good for healing the healers.

Rose quartz offers excellent protection energies during pregnancy and childbirth. This stone is good for the heart and circulatory system, and helps the cleansing organs (liver and kidneys). Rose quartz is associated with the Heart chakra; it helps connect to healing abilities and enhances love.

Sodalite is a stone of logic, rationality, and efficiency. It is helpful for work in groups and stimulates thought. Sodalite is like chicken soup for the energetic soul because it heals head colds quickly and effectively. It is also a cooling stone that is good for burns. This stone will aid sinus inflammation and high blood pressure, and help balance metabolism. Sodalite is great for combating the effects of natural and artificial radiation and is often recommended for those who work around X-ray equipment. This stone relates to the Throat and Brow chakras. During this time of transformation, Sodalite helps one attract like-minded people.

Turquoise is a sacred stone that has been used by Native Americans for centuries in healing work. This stone connects the spiritual bodies with the other three levels: physical, emotional, and intellectual. It is said that turquoise will grow pale on a sickly person but recover its vibrant color when returned to a healthy person. It is connected to the heart and throat energy centers, which in turn connect the three upper and three lower chakras. It is beneficial for the entire body, especially during the many physical and spiritual changes you will encounter during your evolution.

Yellow apatite is a balancing stone that helps integrate the emotional, mental, physical, and spiritual bodies. For this reason it is particularly beneficial as you go through your transformation. It can also be used to clear chakra blockages. It strengthens intuition and, when imbibed as a crystal elixir, suppresses hunger. It can also be programmed as a healing stone to break down the frequency of cellulite and promote smooth skin.

Crystals adjust the vibrations of all the bodily systems. They function as transformers and amplifiers of various energies that rebalance and reenergize your system on the cellular, emotional, mental, and spiritual levels. Crystals and stones are very energy-sensitive and pick up the vibrations from the people who handle them as well as from the general environment. All stones need to be charged, cleansed, and kept away from the frequencies produced by other stones that may compromise their healing abilities. Of course, you should always check with a seasoned, knowledgeable healthcare professional before you start this or any other new healthcare regime.

Bodywork

The fact that you are transforming and evolving does not mean that your physical body should be overlooked. The body is the vehicle that your spirit rides around in, so it must be kept in good working order and in alignment with the new frequency of transformation. Bodywork such as massage and acupressure manipulates and moves the energy of trauma, emotional residue, and long-held cellular memory so you can finally free yourself from the cords that bind.

> Bodywork manipulates and moves the energy of trauma, emotional residue, and long-held cellular memory so you can finally free yourself from the cords that bind.

Massage and acupressure also help eliminate the toxins in your system. As you progress through your transformation, all kinds of aches and pains can arise. Because these changes will come fierce and fast, you must constantly release the accompanying tension and stress until your frequency stabilizes.

The Greek physician Asclepiades of Bithynia (124–40 BC) noted that life itself came from the constant motion of atoms in the body, and that disease and possibly even death were the result of this movement being obstructed or disrupted. Famous American psychic and healer Edgar Cayce recommended natural means of healing and drugless therapies such as diet, rest, and exercise, and the majority of his medical writings recommend massage, with specific techniques targeted at certain ailments. Edgar Cayce believed that the body, mind, and spirit should be treated as a whole entity to insure healing on all levels. For this reason he is considered by many to be the father of holistic medicine.

Acupressure

Acupressure is an ancient healing art that uses pressure on the surface of the skin to stimulate the body's natural self-healing abilities. During an acupressure session certain key points on the body are pressed to release muscular tension, rev up circulation, and get energy moving to aid healing. Acupressure also relaxes the tightened muscles that are so often the result of emotional trauma. Acupressure points are highly conductive, and triggering these points helps reset your changing frequency. There are energy pathways (called *meridians*) that connect the acupressure points to each other and to the internal organs. When these meridians are stimulated they deliver healing energy to all the systems of the body. Acupressure also works on the limbic system, a group of structures in the forebrain where emotions are processed.

> There are pressure points on the skull that can help shift your mind, expand your awareness, and foster psychic insight.

There are actually pressure points on the skull that can help shift your mind, expand your awareness, and foster psychic insight. Another acupressure point located on the brow (where the bridge of the nose meets the forehead) improves intuition when it is activated. Pressing and holding this point clears the mind and facilitates the concentration necessary for staying in the moment, which, as you know, is vital as you go through your psychic evolution. Press and hold the point for at least a minute every day.

Pressing and holding a certain area of the forehead above the eyebrows will help clear and reset your mind. If you draw a straight line up from the center of one of your pupils, you will find an indentation on your forehead about a finger's width from the eyebrow. Press gently on this spot for a minute or so to activate your "reset button." Doing this helps enormously with staying balanced during times of stress. And if you really want to turn the clock back, an acupressure face lift is the way to go. Pressing all of the facial pressure points helps you achieve younger-looking, more toned skin. Acupressure, coupled with the healing properties of yellow apatite crystal (which works on diminishing cellulite), may soon replace liposuction entirely.

Reiki

Reiki is a technique used to heal and balance the subtle energies within your body. Reiki practitioners both administer and act as a channel for energy by a simple laying on of hands. They place their hands on areas where they feel healing energy is most needed. Rather than touching their clients, some Reiki practitioners just hover their hands a few inches above the body, thereby allowing the energy to flow the way it is supposed to and where it is needed the most. Although it is very much about the body, Reiki knows no physical boundaries. A Reiki Master can send healing energy to anyone or anything, anywhere around the world. I personally have experienced long-distance Reiki healing. Remember: In higher consciousness, you are no longer limited by the boundaries of time and space.

> Reiki is a technique used to heal and balance the subtle energies within your body.

Yoga

Yoga is also good for opening up the chakras and tapping into one's psychic senses. Yoga is an ancient physical, mental, and spiritual discipline that helps move vital energy through your chakra system. *Brahmari pranayam* is a breathing rhythm in yoga that is used to improve memory and activate psychic abilities. The Rig Veda, an ancient collection of writings, goes into great detail about the *siddhis*, which are the psychic, magickal, or spiritual powers that arise when the seven major channels of energy throughout the subtle body are opened. By concentrating on the chakras while doing yoga, energy is stimulated to flow through these energy centers. This helps to awaken the corresponding psychic abilities of each chakra and allows the individual to experience higher planes of consciousness.

In Kundalini yoga the practitioner can unite his or her consciousness with Cosmic Consciousness. The Kundalini energy moves up the spine to the chakras and activates them. This is accomplished via the mixing and uniting of *Prana* (cosmic energy) with *Apana* (eliminating energy), which causes pressure and forces Kundalini to rise, again, by means of the Pranayama breathing exercises. Through focus, certain poses, postures, and mantras, the practitioner reaches an altered state of consciousness in which perfect peace, limitless happiness, and enlightenment are the result. Yoga also has many health benefits. It is excellent for treating asthma, high blood pressure, back pain, and arthritis, and is helpful for mental performance, self-awareness, and pain management.

Again, this is hardly an exhaustive list of the treatments available to you. You will find that adapting to the world of energy and frequency will give you many new avenues to pursue for optimum health and healing.

Chi, Within and Without

A good way to keep the energy flowing in your environment is to use feng shui, the ancient Chinese practice of placement and arrangement in order to achieve harmony between people and their environment. It is also a good idea to create some sacred space within your home that serves as a sanctuary for you. It's important to take time off from all of those computers and cell phones and their attendant electromagnetic frequencies. Remember that planet Earth is shifting along with you and is therefore going through her own "detox" from pollutants and negative energies. Earth has her own chakra centers or energy vortices that will respond in kind to the types of frequencies we feed her. The rebirth of our planet encompasses the complete package of caring for the environment, stopping the pollution of our air and water, and, above all else, raising the vibration from the collective consciousness. It is vital for the well-being of our planet that we become more sensitive to and aware of how we live. Going Green by recycling, eschewing plastic bags, driving a hybrid car (or, better yet, walking or cycling), using solar and wind power—all of these things, although small acts of an individual, will in the long run help to keep Earth in balance and evolving right along with us.

You Are What (Frequency) You Eat

Now more than ever you will be influenced by the frequencies of the foods you eat. Organic food is free of pesticides, preservative, and hormones, and has a vibration more conducive to your new lighter spirit body. By eating organic you will find it easier to ensure optimum health. Being mindful and educated about what you eat, where it comes from, how it was grown or raised, and how your own body transforms it into energy will help you feed your newly awakened, energy-sensitive body, mind, and spirit. Ditch your microwave and nourish yourself with foods in their natural state. Microwaves heat food by creating molecular friction, and this friction breaks down essential vitamins and naturally occurring phytonutrients (plant medicines). One study showed that microwaving vegetables destroys up to 97 percent of their nutritional content—the very vitamins and nutrients that prevent disease, boost immune function, and enhance health. You will find that your newly opened extrasensory senses will function better when the vibrations from your food are in harmony with your chakra centers. Red meat can dull your psychic perception because it has a heavy vibration and takes a long time to digest. Limit the amount of red meat that you eat because it has a very desensitizing effect on your psychic empathy. Remember

> The rebirth of our planet encompasses the complete package of caring for the environment, stopping the pollution of our air and water, and, above all else, raising the vibration from the collective consciousness.

also that the way in which an animal is treated and slaughtered will register as a vibration in the meat you buy at the supermarket.

Now that we've covered some of the basics concerning diet, here are some specific dietary recommendations for each of your chakras. If you put sludge into your car's gas tank, it won't run; the same goes for your transformed body and its vital energy centers, the chakras. In order for them to keep spinning and filtering energy properly, you must maintain them with the right fuel. Of course, always consult with a healthcare professional before making any changes to your diet, particularly if you have food allergies or known sensitivities to certain foods.

Root chakra fuel: Root vegetables such as carrots, potatoes, parsnips, radishes, beets, and onions are good for your Root chakra. These foods will help keep you grounded as you venture into your newly opened psychic areas of consciousness. The Root chakra requires some protein from meat at times, but eggs, beans, tofu, soy products, and nuts can nourish this energy center as well. You can even spice things up with horseradish, hot paprika, chives, cayenne pepper, and black or white pepper.

Sacral chakra fuel: Your Sacral chakra (and your creativity) is best nourished with sweet fruits such as melons, mangos, strawberries, oranges, and coconuts. Honey, almonds, and walnuts dashed with some cinnamon are sure to keep your creative energy swirling.

Solar Plexus chakra fuel: Feeding this chakra helps support your self-esteem, especially given the number of changes and detachments that will be occurring during the energy shift. Granola, pasta, bread, cereal, rice, and sunflower seeds will give you comfort naturally. Yogurt spiced with some ginger or mint is also a good choice.

Heart chakra fuel: Now that your psychic empathy is making you more prone to picking up on the emotional hurts and discomforts of others, it is important to keep this chakra fortified with the proper nutrients. Your Heart chakra needs leafy vegetables such as spinach, kale, and dandelion greens, and vegetables such as broccoli, cauliflower, cabbage, celery, and squash. Green tea is the perfect beverage because it contains antioxidants that are good for the heart. (I wonder if Simon and Garfunkel knew about the Heart chakra's ideal herbs: parsley, sage, rosemary, and thyme.)

Throat chakra fuel: Your Throat chakra (and your ability to speak your authentic truth) will benefit from eating tart or tangy fruits such as lemons, limes, grapefruits, or kiwis. Apples, plums, pears, peaches, and apricots are also good fruits for Throat chakra maintenance. Drink plenty of liquids, especially purified water, along with fruit juices and herbal teas. Sodium has a crystalline form that resonates with this chakra, so pass the sea salt (much better than table salt)!

Third Eye/Brow chakra fuel: The awakened Brow chakra requires plenty of dark-colored fruits such as blueberries, red grapes, blackberries, and raspberries. Red wine is also great for this chakra. Lavender is a very soothing herb that will help ease the headache that is often experienced as this psychic chakra center begins to function at full force.

Crown chakra fuel: To aid the spiritual communication center for your newly transformed self, it is a good idea to fast occasionally. Fasting and detoxing will help keep this higher channel clear so you can make a strong connection with the higher dimension of consciousness. Incense and smudging herbs such as sage, copal, myrrh, frankincense, and juniper will help keep your space in the higher realms of frequency.

Eighth chakra fuel: This chakra is nourished solely by the vibrations from your thoughts and the purity of unconditional love. Its element is ether, the medium for transmission of electromagnetic waves.

Diaphragm/"Buddha Belly" chakra fuel: In order to breathe freely and purposefully, you should avoid foods that give you acid reflux and gas. This chakra will sometimes crave sugar and salt upon awakening, so be mindful of your intake so that you don't create an imbalance. Smoking greatly impairs this chakra.

Thymus chakra fuel: A diet rich in fruits and vegetables will support this newly awakened chakra center. It is also a good idea to bolster the thymus with peppermint, garlic, oranges, and lemon peel.

There are countless healing modalities for the newly transformed body, including everything we've already covered here as well as color healing, sound healing, tuning forks, and magnetic therapy, just to name a few. The most effective healing method, however, is the one that is powered by your own thoughts. Your evolution will give you the power to heal yourself and others. Have you ever asked yourself why some people succumb to a particular illness, while others in the same situation recover? It comes down to one's mental attitude and belief system, and the power of one's thoughts. Your thoughts affect your body's cells, which then vibrate and send off electromagnetic waves. The more you concentrate on a particular thought or thoughts, the greater the vibrations of the cells. The electromagnetic waves, in turn, encode the message that you are sending into your cells until it becomes strong enough to manifest as a reality. Positive thinking can raise your vibration as much as 10 Hz, whereas negative thinking can lower your vibration by as much as 15 Hz.

The most effective healing method is the one that is powered by your own thoughts. Your evolution will give you the power to heal yourself and others.

The power of your thoughts is your strongest medicine.

Frequency Boosters: Do You Want a New Drug?

Some people are so anxious to get through their transformation that they experiment with certain substances that open them up psychically. This really isn't a good idea if you are not aware of how psychic energy flows and works with the chakra centers. The wrong substance in the wrong amount at the wrong time can leave you drained, physically ill, mentally disturbed, and wide open for psychic attack. Two of the most popular substances are white powder gold (monoatomic gold) and Ayahuasca, a mind-altering brew containing DMT (dimethyltryptamine, a naturally occurring psychedelic), also known as the spirit molecule.

White powder gold was the elixir of the ancients. They knew that it could enhance one's manifesting abilities, promote a youthful appearance, correct health problems, and take the user on quite an enlightenment trip. It enabled them to experience expanded consciousness and ignited their extrasensory senses. The Egyptian Book of the Dead makes reference to a hyper-dimensional realm called the Field of Mfkzt, which is an ethereal plane accessible only through the use of gold that has been transformed. There is a special process by which gold and other metals can be turned into a single atom (or monatomic substance): a form of powder that has superconductive properties. Laurence Gardner stated in his book *Lost Secrets of the Sacred Ark* that monoatomic gold was the secret of the pharaohs' rite of passage to the Afterlife. In alchemy it is referred to as the Philosopher's Stone or the Elixir of Life. It is thought to bring about ultimate knowledge and the gift of perpetual youth. Even Harry Potter knows about it! Was the Golden Fleece of ancient Greece, the fleece sought after by Jason, really just a metaphor for white powder gold? Fleeces were connected with high magick and alchemy during that time, and many folk traditions continue to maintain that belief.

> The wrong substance in the wrong amount at the wrong time can leave you drained, physically ill, mentally disturbed, and wide open for psychic attack.

White powder gold excludes all external magnetic fields (including Earth's gravity) and takes you on a trip beyond the third and fourth dimensional space-time continuum, bringing you to fifth-dimensional consciousness. This is the dimension of imagination where your thoughts manifest; here, you're capable of levitation, teleportation, telepathy, and amazing psychic feats. White powder gold does all this by changing your frequency. You tune in to the channel of higher consciousness to bring about personal transformation. Shifting your frequency to a higher level enables you to move into higher dimensions, where you can experience your lighter and more psychic makeup. The problem with white powder gold is that it also enhances manifestation abilities. If you aren't careful, negative intentions will take form and come about in an instant. It also completely alters your chakra frequencies; if you aren't balanced and aligned in all energy areas, you can really create problems for yourself. This would be akin to trying to tune up your car and having no idea what you are doing; you'll cause more problems than you fix. Clearly this is not something to play around with.

Ayahuasca is another substance that is sought after by people who are so anxious to leave the limited three-dimensional consciousness that they attempt to "induce" their rebirth into the higher dimensions of expanded awareness. Ayahuasca is a visionary concoction that has been used ritually by shamans and the indigenous peoples of the Amazon basin for centuries, for prophecy, divination, telepathy, shape-shifting, cleansing, diagnosis of illnesses, and healing. The brew is a combination of the *Banisteriopsis caapi* vine and DMT-containing plants. It can jettison you on an expanding consciousness trip that can last up to four or five hours. The DMT works with the pineal gland and brings about extreme psychic and visionary experiences. As your energy/spirit body moves beyond the third-dimensional realms of time and space, you feel what it is like to function from the various psychic centers or chakras.

In his book *DMT: The Spirit Molecule*, Rick Strassman proposed that the release of DMT from the pineal gland precisely 49 days after conception marks the spirit's entrance into the body of the fetus. This 49-day prenatal period corresponds to the first signs of fetal pineal tissue, as well as the determination of the baby's sex. According to Tibetan Buddhist tradition, this same time period also corresponds to the time between the death of an individual and that soul's next re-birth or incarnation. Strassman suggests that the individual's life-force enters the body through the pineal gland and also leaves through the pineal gland at the time of death. Many people who have had near-death experiences (NDEs)

> Tune in to the channel of higher consciousness to bring about personal transformation.

describe feeling completely disconnected from their physical bodies and functioning from a perspective above that of three-dimensional consciousness. Many also report enhanced psychic sensory perceptions and sightings of spirits, sometimes even the Ascended Masters. Some NDEs can be disturbing when the emotion of fear has not completely dissolved. This brings about the sensation of being stuck in the lower dimensions and can put one in contact with evil beings, loud noises, disembodied voices, and human spirits in distress. Some people see spirits of those who have already passed on who seem to be acting as guides who help them cross over into the light. Strassman advanced the theory that a massive release of DMT from the pineal gland prior to death or near-death was the cause of the expanded consciousness experience.

An Ayahuasca experience can be quite enlightening; it can also be extremely disturbing and even dangerous because you are opening yourself up to lower energies and even the risk of possession. In order to pass through to the higher realms you sometimes have to go through the lower levels of consciousness that hold demonic energies and disembodied thought-forms. Some people have reported a feeling of being attacked by large animals while experimenting with Ayahuasca before being properly educated and aware of the dynamics of frequency. In addition, suddenly realizing that the physical world is one big illusion can be very disturbing if you are not prepared for this information. In this way an Ayahuasca trip is similar to an induced near-death experience. You are in a kind of psychic free-fall in which you have no control over what you experience because you are not grounded in any one reality. You are experiencing total, unfettered expanded consciousness.

> Suddenly realizing that the physical world is one big illusion can be very disturbing.

The empowering shift will ignite your psychic awareness naturally, *without* the help of any substances. Prematurely trying to enter the realms of higher consciousness without the right frequencies flowing through your chakra centers can introduce fear into your system, which can hinder your evolution as you process that heavy emotional energy. Again, the best thing to do is to go through your transformation naturally and embrace the gestation and rebirth of the enlightened you as it occurs.

The Changing Roles of Psychics, Mediums, and Astrologers

The most notable transformation you will undergo as part of your evolution is the opening up of your innate psychic abilities. This can be a very exciting time as well as a very confusing time. Tuning in to your telepathy now gives you the insight that was once only the purview of gifted psychics, mediums, and enlightened mystics. I have spent the greater part of this life (and many other lives as well) as an astrologer and psychic counselor. For years I've tried to get my clients to realize that I don't write their news; I only report it. Everything that you think and imagine becomes your reality, and when you are stuck in three-dimensional consciousness, that reality usually involves quite a bit of emotional drama. Before the empowering

> Tuning in to your telepathy now gives you the insight that was once only the purview of gifted psychics, mediums, and enlightened mystics.

shift, most of us created and related primarily to chaos and drama, and attached ourselves to the material things that falsely defined us as we continued to try to make sense of life. In ego consciousness we sought to control and "one-up" others so we could feel empowered. We consulted psychics, mediums, and astrologers because we wanted to know what the future held; maybe we wanted a probable outcome concerning a relationship, our money, our health, or our career. We were in search of quick-fix answers.

Times are changing. You are now plugged in to the Divine force that is the source of all guidance, so the answers you seek come from within, not without. Now, consulting a psychic is more about how to get rid of the static in your own energy field so you can heal yourself and create your own reality. In my first book, *The Street Smart Psychic's Guide to*

Getting a Good Reading, I explained how psychics work with energy to help their clients decode the reality that they have created for themselves. In the old consciousness, psychics were erroneously thought of merely as fortune-tellers. The truth is that they are spiritual "first responders." Psychics certainly have their work cut out for them, especially with those clients who have difficulty during the Crowning phase of their transformation into higher consciousness. Detaching from things that no longer serve your highest good and cleaning out the emotional baggage from your consciousness closet can leave you feeling very lost and confused, especially when you start adding things like synchronicities, lucid dreams, psychic impressions, and repeating number patterns into the mix. Psychics and lightworkers help you make sense of these uncanny events until you become accustomed to living in the higher vibrations of awareness.

You are now plugged into the Divine force that is the source of all guidance.

Psychics help you learn the different methods of grounding so you can more easily manipulate energy. An experienced psychic will tell you that thoughts of love and healing energy manifest the quickest because they come from a higher, more refined frequency. Conversely, manipulative, controlling, or possessive thoughts disguised as love can actually repel the intended target, particularly if he or she is evolved and can sense the real intentions behind telepathic messages. He or she can then simply block out the unwanted messages.

Tarot cards and the frequencies of number patterns in numerology are often helpful in finding answers to your psychic questions. Crystals, especially quartz crystals, are another excellent way to tap into the transmissions of frequencies from the upper realms. Anything that you can link into vibrationally can be used as a tool to stimulate and hone your psychic senses. Eventually your telepathic abilities will become sufficiently refined and vigorous to enable you to tap into the frequency waves of the universe without any outside help. Awareness and mindfulness will be the only two things you'll need to successfully pick up and decode the messages residing in the energy all around you. The veil of separation is gone. You have the gift of second sight, the all-seeing eye, which was revered by our ancient ancestors, the extraterrestrial visitors and colonizers who, as I've already noted, are very much a part of our hidden history.

> Thoughts of love and healing energy manifest the quickest because they come from a higher, more refined frequency.

Psychic Mediums

As you begin to access the higher levels of spiritual awareness, you will be put into contact with energy beings and spirits who have passed over. When this happens, you may want the guidance from a seasoned psychic medium. Michael Tottey, a brilliant psychic medium who lives in the United Kingdom, has said that he has taken on the role of teacher and healer for his clients, rather than that of predictor or oracle. Now that the psychic evolution is under way, more and more people are beginning to understand that these abilities are a natural part of their awakened, transformed energy system. Michael acts more as a rebirthing coach—a doula, if you will—who helps walk his clients through some of the things they can expect to experience as their psychic senses open up and come to fruition. Michael is an old soul who has been around for a very long time. His mediumship abilities are uncanny, particularly when it comes to connecting with spirits residing on the other side of the veil. People who aren't accustomed to being clairvoyant and clairaudient often become upset when they first encounter such spirits or imprinted energy, whether positive or negative. Michael feels that his new mission is to show these people how to accept and embrace this new way of sensing, as well as to teach the importance of psychic protection and grounding. Staying protected and grounded is very important when you first begin to open up psychically, or else you risk going into a free fall of clairvoyant chaos. Michael fears that some people who have not been properly educated about spirit energy may at first behave like children with new toys and play around with psychic energy irresponsibly. Because they are now dealing with pure energy, any frivolous use of psychic abilities can leave them wide open for psychic burnout, in which their energy is depleted or, in the worst-case scenario, they are possessed by an entity or thought-form.

Michael stresses that the shift that is ushering in our evolution is not about everything being great and wonderful. It also involves having superior awareness, and part of that awareness means that you will now have first-hand knowledge of the dark energies existing in the "murk" of the universe. Michael teaches his protégés to always make sure they aren't dealing with a lower vibration or trickster spirit. Antagonistic entities like to play games with psychic ingénues. Michael instructs his clients on the best methods for connecting with their spirit guides. These guides act as energetic bodyguards as you venture into the dark alleys and unsavory areas of the frequency realms.

It is also very common for psychic newcomers to confuse ghost energy with spirit energy. According to Michael (who has been on hundreds of ghost hunts), ghost energy is a shadowy, residual energy that is tethered to Earth's plane by strong emotional connecting cords. Areas that are subject to hauntings usually have stone or granite floors or walls that contain silica, a substance with a crystalline form that is known to record and hold the frequencies from potent emotions—for example, those surrounding a beheading or a murder. Sometimes these sorts of ghostly energies can be cleared, but some are too firmly entrenched and trapped within the walls of echoing resonance. Michael notes that the human body is a natural energy generator; it produces 2.2 kilowatts of electricity per day—enough to run a small electrical fire for a short amount of time. We already know that energy can't be destroyed, only changed, so when the energy from these kinds of strong emotions gets trapped, you can imagine the intensity of the resulting frequency, which we then label as a haunting.

> Ghost energy is a shadowy, residual energy tethered to Earth's plane by strong emotional cords.

Your newfound abilities will allow you to tune in to what Michael calls *intelligent ghosts* or *spirits*. Such ghosts usually want to convey a message or offer help. They also respect boundaries and will not interfere with free will, so you are free to choose whether or not you will accept their help. Michael himself is able to contact those who have passed over; he finds that it is often comforting for clients to know that deceased loved ones still live on but in a different form. Michael emphasizes the fact that your transformation will require a great deal of discernment in the use of your newly opened psychic abilities, because negative spirit attachments can require the expertise of an exorcist. An exorcist is trained in the practice of casting out negative spiritual entities from a person or place that they have possessed. So enter this new world with awareness, respect, good intentions, and the proper protections in place. You are playing with the big boys now!

Astrology: Your GPS for the Cosmos

Courteous Reader, Astrology is one of the most ancient Sciences, held in high esteem of old, by the Wise and the Great. Formerly, no Prince would make War or Peace, nor any General fight in Battle, in short, no important affair was undertaken without first consulting an Astrologer.
—Benjamin Franklin

Benjamin Franklin was a great American statesman and, in my opinion, an advanced being who was reincarnated throughout history so that humanity could benefit from his knowledge and expertise. He was wise enough to view astrology as an instrument for guidance, a way to navigate probable outcomes based on the interplay of frequencies among the planets, the stars, and the luminaries, such as the moon. The Emerald Tablet, also called the Secret of Hermès, is a short work from which we derive the phrase "As above, so below"—a succinct declaration that reveals the secret of the elemental substances that influenced creation. What all this means is that the cosmos above us has a direct effect on our daily existence. As you go through your transformation you will realize that this knowledge of the stars and planets (given to us by higher beings) is actually a very useful and pragmatic tool to help you understand the vibrational world of the galaxy. It is also a very old tool: In the Book of Enoch I, one of the oldest history books in existence, the angel Baraqel teaches the human race about astrology, and Kokabel, another angel, instructs us how to use it. Sariel, one of the seven archangels (originally listed in the Enoch books as Saraqel), teaches of the courses of the moon, which was at one time regarded as forbidden knowledge.

The stars and planets exert a direct vibrational pull on us. Just as the wind can buffet you and a blistering summer sun can burn you, so do the cosmic elements exert their influence on your life. The different chakra centers and the organs of your physical body all resonate with the frequencies of the heavenly bodies, with the moon having the strongest effect on most people because it governs intuition. It is through the vital centers or chakras that the planets influence the human system. During your transformation you will react to the new planetary vibrations being pulled in due to Earth's position in the Milky Way galaxy. Consulting an astrologer will help you understand what planetary and stellar frequencies you are tuning in to and how to work with the energy of the heavens in order to fully evolve to a state of higher consciousness. A trained astrologer will explain to you how your astrological birth chart can help you negate past karma, make energy corrections, and reach the next level of evolution by working with the frequency that is available to you during specific planetary transits. The houses of the birth chart show what aspects of your current incarnation are in a stage of development or resolution. Additionally, each sign of the zodiac relates to certain body part and level of consciousness.

As the Earth moves through the Milky Way, the procession of the zodiac changes. As of this writing we are leaving the Piscean age and going into the Aquarian age. Currently we use 12 signs in the astrological birth chart, but New Thought astrology often includes the sign of Ophiuchus (pronounced *off-ee-YOO-kuhs*) because it is relevant to our transformation into the higher dimensions of consciousness. (Early cultures based their yearly calendar on 13 lunar cycles of 28 days each; our present Julian Calendar consists of only 12 months: the 13th month and its correspond- ing astrological sign were removed during the time of Julius Caesar.) Ophiuchus is a large constellation located just northwest of the center of the Milky Way. It is one of the 88 known constellations as well as one of the original 48 listed by Ptolemy. Ophiuchus is symbolized by the Snake Charmer or Serpent Wrestler, a man handling a serpent and dividing the large snake into two parts. (We know this symbol today as the Staff of Asclepius, the medical symbol.) Some astrologers believe the planetoid Chiron, which is connected with healing in Greek mythology, is the rul- er of this sign of short duration. The sign of Ophiuchus was fashioned after the original serpent holder, Enki, a Sumerian god associated with water, crafts, intelligence, and the creation of humanity. The sun spends only 19 days in this sign. It falls between Scorpio and Sagittarius, the natural eighth house of physical death, and the ninth house of spiritual- ity and the higher mind, respectively. The constellation of Ophiuchus is the only sign of the zodiac linked to a real person. This person, Imhotep, lived in Egypt around the 27th century BC. Imhotep is credited with many accomplishments, including the knowledge and use of medicine. It is believed that Nostradamus used the constellation of Ophiuchus while making his astrological predictions. Interestingly Nostradmus was not only a seer and an astrologer: He was also a physician.

So what does this 13th sign of the zodiac have to do with our trans- formation and evolution? There has been much controversy surrounding this sign, but the reality is that it contains the as- trological clues to our evolution and trans- formation into higher awareness. The new vibrations from the cosmos will activate our additional DNA, which will give us access to the secrets and mysteries of who we are and what our purpose is, as well as the higher dimensions of frequency that exist beyond the Earthly plane. Our DNA,

> The new vibrations from the cosmos will activate our additional DNA, which will give us access to the secrets and mysteries of who we are and what our purpose is.

with its double-helix structure, is often associated with the *Ouroboros*, an ancient alchemical symbol depicting a snake or dragon swallowing its own tail, forming an endless circle and constantly re-creating itself. In some representations, the serpent is half light and half dark, reminiscent of the Tao symbol of yin and yang, which shows the dual nature—positive and negative, male and female, light and dark—of all things.

The "12 around 1" pattern (12 = 1 + 2 = 3) represents the third dimension, or what we experience as physical reality—that which is based in linear time and the world of cause and effect. This is where our spirit experiences the physical world. In the third dimension the vibrations of our thoughts and emotions slow down so that we can actually see what we hold in our consciousness. However, much of who we are becomes lost in this dimension of limits and constraints. And so we mark time in cycles and patterns. We find this "12 around 1" pattern on our clocks, our calendars, the zodiac wheel, the alchemical wheel, the wheel of time, and in karma itself. Could the sign of Ophiuchus, which falls strategically between the zodiac's eighth house (sex, death, and regeneration) and ninth house (the higher mind and spirituality), be the linking sign for the knowledge we need to upgrade our DNA and advance to the next level of consciousness? If so, our lesson might also be to understand that, through physical death, there is rebirth.

The symbolism of the number 13 is of great significance in several cultures and religions. The 12 disciples and Christ formed a group of 13 to share in the Last Supper. In ancient Greece, Zeus was counted as the 13th and most powerful god. The symbolism of 13 especially comes into play in the story of Osiris, the Egyptian god of life, death, and powerful cosmic energy who was murdered by his brother, Typhon, who then sliced him into 14 pieces. Isis, Osiris's wife and sister, could find only 13 of the 14 body parts (the missing part being the generative organ, which fell into the Nile and was eaten by a school of fish). This story illustrates that the number 13 is the precursor to completion, a fact that is also borne out by nature itself. There are 13 moons in a calendar year. The moon is associated with the Spiral of Life—birth, death, and rebirth—as she moves through the phases from dark to full and back to dark again.

In the Tarot, the number 13 is represented by the Death card, which signifies transition and change. Could our over-looked 13th sign of the zodiac become even more significant as we move beyond the empowering shift? Will we eventually be able to understand the healing vibrations coming from this constellation? I believe that

> The number 13 is the precursor to completion.

this will be the next phase of cosmic energy that will be made available to us in the higher psychic dimensions. This is where we will fine-tune our chakras and begin to heal ourselves as we strive for harmony with the Divine creative force of the universe. Astrologers can provide you with the necessary information concerning the lessons associated with each astrological sign, as well as how to work with the different planetary frequencies.

At the center of the Milky Way galaxy, the Galactic Center, there is a group of stars surrounding a black hole. Our planet is moving toward an eventual alignment with that Galactic Center, the wormhole (read: birth canal) through which we will be birthed—rebirthed, really—into a new dimension of consciousness and finally brought into contact with our galactic neighbors. It is these galactic neighbors to whom we will finally turn our attention in the next, final chapter.

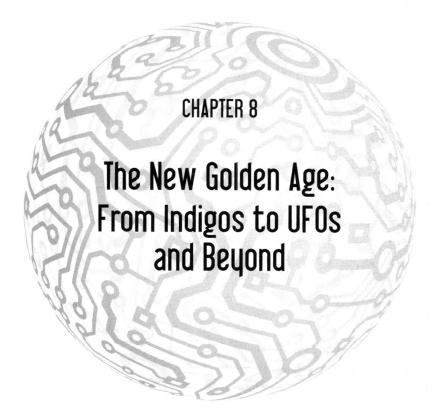

CHAPTER 8

The New Golden Age: From Indigos to UFOs and Beyond

As our solar system transitions from the Age of Pisces (illusion and religious dogma) to the Age of Aquarius (advanced, intuitive technology; humanitarianism; and outer space), our consciousness will be tuning in to a higher frequency in a process that our creators and the great civilizations of the past—particularly the Maya—had long foretold. The part of our DNA that codes to the spirit gene was deactivated centuries ago for fear that we would misuse the advanced psychic aspect of our nature. The "fall" of humanity into the lower dimensions of consciousness meant that we were trapped for centuries under the veil of false illusions that blocked any activating light or energy. Earth's electromagnetic grids were held captive by the heavy, negative fear vibrations, which were mirrored back down to us as reversals and illusions. The illusions "worked" for a time because multiple sources of information were pitted against each other to cause confusion, and with confusion there can be no light, no clarity. These conflicting sources of information left

201

the human race completely at the mercy of matter because reality was based only on what could be experienced with the five senses.

The gig is up. Due to the precession of the equinox into the constellation of Aquarius, the dormant codes within our DNA will now automatically be tuned in and turned on to the brighter light and frequency coming into the world as part of this amazing transformation. Our perception will now be guided by our internal psychic source, allowing us to see the truth that transcends all physical matter. The electromagnetic grids on our planet will also be altered and refined, which will inspire our spiritual evolution. This shift will outshine all fear. Fear will not diminish completely, but we will now be able to understand and manipulate it as a frequency instead of a fact. We can dial down the volume of this harmful frequency in the same way that we turn down our radio or iPod. The Age of Piscean illusion and magicians gives way to the golden Age of Aquarius as we embark on a spiritual journey that awakens the true spiritual mystic in all of us. Our enslavement to the material world will finally end as we evolve and wake up to remember who we really are: spirits from one ultimate Source. This is the end of materialism as we know it.

The source of this upgrade will be the stellar frequency package of Aquarius, comprising Alpha Aquarii (Sadalmelik), a supergiant star with a diameter 100 times that of the sun; Beta Aquarii (Sadalsund), the brightest single star of the constellation, shining at magnitude 2.9; and Gamma Aquarii (Sadachbia), a spectroscopic binary that shines at magnitude 3.8.[1] Their Arabic names translate as "luck of the king," "luck of lucks," and "lucky star of hidden things," respectively. These three

---

1. Magnitude is a measurement of how bright a star *appears to be* in our sky. Although this measurement tells us how bright each star appears it does not tell us how bright a star actually is. This is because all stars are at different distances from us: Those nearer appear brighter and those farther away appear less bright.

Beta Aquarii is brighter than its constellation-mate, Alpha Aquarii, only because it is 140 light years closer to us.

Spectroscopic binaries (such as Gamma Aquarii) are systems in which the stars are so close together that they appear as a single star even in a telescope.

> The dormant codes within our DNA will now automatically be turned on to the brighter light and frequency coming into the world.

heavenly bodies combine to create the luminosity of about 25 suns. The intensity of this light will further activate our additional strands of DNA. It may even allow scientists to identify the "spirit code" or "God gene" in our genetic makeup.

The first computers were the precursors to the lightening-fast communication we now enjoy when we surf the Web or e-mail our friends. Now, through your advanced senses, you will be able to connect telepathically to the world-wide consciousness. Ultimately telepathy will replace all other means of communication. We *are* the new technology. This is all very Aquarian. (On a related note, I wonder if the 1960s musical group The Fifth Dimension understood the synchronicity inherent in their name, or that it is the dimension associated with the Age of Aquarius.)

From Separateness to Unity

Planet Earth and her inhabitants will once again experience life as it was before the "fall," when humanity was thrust into the abyss of the lower dimensions of consciousness. The higher band of frequency coming into Earth's atmosphere is enticing and magnetic, and will fill the world with a new energy. Once you begin to sense how you can move and flow with energy you will never again want to go backward and attach yourself to the slower, dense energy of matter. Matter will still exist, and your physical body will still function in a material world, but you will now be driven by a higher, more psychic creative consciousness. You are like a baby all over again, learning to make your way in and even manipulate this new world of energy for the very first time. You will finally see our planet as part of a larger cosmos made up of magnetic forces, bands of

> We are all part of one amazing living organism that spans to infinity.

frequencies, and layers of consciousness; we are all part of one amazing living organism that spans to infinity. As our awareness increases we see that there is no separateness, because the self and the Source of self are one and the same. Once you open up and connect with nature and your environment, everything speaks and communicates to you through the telepathic frequency waves of the universe. Your transformation will allow you to experience the interconnectedness of everything.

Social and Cultural Changes

> Lightworkers will be the new social workers.

This transformative upgrade will have a direct impact on how we function as a society. In keeping with the vibration and temperament of the Age of Aquarius, society will become ever more creative, technologically advanced, progressive, psychic, and unique. The transformation will open up myriad new jobs and careers to serve the needs of a more advanced society. You can expect a steep rise in the number of jobs in alternative health, supertechnology, and various psychic disciplines. This is also a climate in which creative conceptual artists and inventors will flourish. Lightworkers will be the new social workers, and humanitarian efforts will be fueled by the collective consciousness that recognizes that we are all linked to each other and the main Source, the universe.

Education will embrace more of a balance between left brain and right brain. The schooling of "special needs" children will also undergo a radical alteration, as we now know that they are telepathic and psychically attuned rather than "slow" or "challenged." Teachers will be dealing with students who see the answers even before they see the questions on exams; cheating will become a thing of the past. Cyberschooling may become a trend due to the extreme sensitivity of these children. Until grounding and aura protection are fully mastered, exposure to group energy can be overwhelming for them. Schools will teach the true history of our planet, to include information about our ancient ancestors, the real galactic explorers that seeded and colonized Earth. Geography class will teach where the great civilizations of Atlantis and Lemuria once were, and how they are still accessible through the spirit's ability to astrally project. Imagine school field trips to these locations via group teleportation!

Spirituality

The more psychic we become the more we will want to expose and break down the false structures and beliefs that have held us down for so long. The Indigos did a wonderful job of starting the process, and now is the time for us to embrace our extrasensory spiritual nature and move into the flow of the new vibrations. The great Ascended Masters, such as Jesus, John the Baptist, Buddha, Saint Germaine, and Shiva, just to name a few, will all be recognized as teachers of the same universal truth of love, peace, and unity. The religious separateness that was once the cause of many wars will give way to a unified spirituality as we become aware of our mutual Source. These Masters wanted us to realize that love raises our consciousness because it has the highest vibration and initiates healing on every level—physical, emotional, and spiritual. With our new consciousness we will finally be able to put aside the differences that were created out of and nurtured by fear. Just as every rose on a rose bush is slightly different but nonetheless part of the same plant, the rebirth of the world into a new golden age enables us to transcend the notion of separateness in favor of sensing the uniqueness *and* diversity of the one Source from which everything originates. We no longer have to operate within a system that compartmentalizes and separates everything; instead, our advanced awareness encourages us to help one another as opposed to always

> The rebirth of the world into a new golden age enables us to transcend the notion of separateness in favor of sensing the uniqueness and diversity of the one Source from which everything originates.

competing and comparing. Religious, racial, and cultural wars, all fueled by greed, propaganda, and fear, will serve as reminders for us to never sink back into the depths lower consciousness.

Given that we are now fully aware of how the universe communicates to us through frequency, we will gain a new respect for the art of astrology. Once considered an esoteric art meant for the gifted few, it will become an everyday practice. Acknowledging the fact that our ancient ancestors came from one of those star systems or planets that share space with us in the vast heavens will allow us to finally drop our Earth-centered arrogance.

Healthcare

We will open up to the amazing benefits of vibrational medicine as the type of healthcare that is most suited to our highly attuned physio-psychic system. Integrated medicine will be a combination of scientific Western medicine and holistic treatments because we understand that disease in the physical body is always rooted in the frequency of the subtle body. Eventually centers for chakra system programming and balancing will be as common as hair salons. Our innate ability to heal from within will be "remembered" as we integrate vibrational medicine with the technology that was and is still being given to us by our extraterrestrial emissaries. Our views on death and dying will also be completely reconfigured because we know that frequency supersedes and ultimately transcends matter. Many holy books claim that at the time of the passing of the old Earth into a new Earth, the dead will rise from their graves. What this actually means is that because of our awareness of spirit energy, we will not experience death in the same way once we are in higher consciousness. We know that there is more to life than height, weight, and depth; the fear of facing our own mortality will be a thing of the past because in higher consciousness, we identify primarily with the vibrational body instead of the physical one.

> The fear of facing our own mortality will be a thing of the past.

Your spirit essence will see its work done as one identity and eventually move into another aspect of its personality.

A New Environmentalism

As we become more attuned and linked to the vibrations around us, a renewed respect for the environment will emerge. We will more readily embrace the use of natural energy alternatives such as solar, wind, and even psychic energy power. This will lessen our dependence on oil, the lifeblood of our planet. Architects will take advantage of these natural energy sources and thus design buildings that will be more conducive to living in a world of higher vibrations. New homes will be built in the shape of a pyramid because pyramids collect subtle energy and transfer it easily to our own frequency. Pyramids are known for having an anti-aging effect on whatever is inside them; this alone should make staying home more beneficial than going to the gym. The intensity of Alpha waves also increases inside pyramids; this will help keep residents relaxed and effortlessly alert, a great combination for staying in the Now moment. Pyramids also charge energy, so communication via transmitting telepathic messages over long distances will be easier inside these new homes. They may even boast built-in sound and color systems that will help their owners reboot their vibrational levels should they fall short. Imagine a room that is programmed to change color according to the frequency that is needed in order for you to stay physically, mentally, and psychically attuned. Think of the business opportunities that will arise for real estate developers, architects, and interior designers!

Politics

The rebirth of the world doesn't guarantee that you will live in a Utopian society. Remember: The lower vibrations still exist. Your evolution and extrasensory advancement will merely make you *more aware* of these lower energies so you can better protect yourself from anyone or anything that could compromise your well-being. You will still be functioning in a physical world, and not everyone will be evolving at the same rate; some won't evolve at all. Fortunately, our transformation will bring us into a vibration that leads to peacefulness and humanitarianism.

We will need to be governed by leaders who are in tune with the morals and ethics that support higher consciousness. The leaders of the rebirthed world will have positions that resemble diplomatic advisory positions more than actual leadership roles. Organized councils will oversee different arms of the government, instead of autocrats and power-mongers who are operating under the mistaken assumption that they alone hold authority. This is not a One World Order as much as it is a One World Consciousness that will connect all of Earth's inhabitants. Of course, our admission into the Galactic Society means that being vigilant about the intentions of our alien neighbors will be more of a priority.

Technology

One of the most anticipated events of the empowering shift is the opening of the stargates that will allow us to travel to other worlds. These portals were shut down after the "fall" of humanity, but upon our awakening transformation, we will once again have access to the galactic communities that have been watching and waiting for this moment. The many scientific and technological breakthroughs and advances of the 20th century were given to us by advanced alien beings in order to help our planet survive the empowering shift into the Aquarian Age and help socialize us in the new galactic community. Some of our biggest advances have come from the retro-engineering of UFO technology. It will soon be possible to communicate with beings from distant star systems; wormholes into parallel universes and stargates will once again be accessible to us; and the pineal gland will become our personal stargate portal, making time travel and astral projection possible.

> One of the most anticipated events of the empowering shift is the opening of the stargates that will allow us to travel to other worlds.

Portals into other dimensions, such as those that lie on the Bermuda Triangle; at the Puerta de Hayu Marca (gate of the gods), deep within the Andes Mountains of Peru; at the Dragon's Triangle, near Japan; and at the location of the ancient Sumerian city of Ur, in southern Iraq, were and likely still are the doorways through which our ancient alien ancestors entered our realm. Many new portals like these will open up as we move into the Photon Belt and Age of Aquarius. This will enable us to travel to other worlds and parallel universes. Earth was once at the outer edge or "suburbs" of the Milky Way galaxy; now it is moving ever closer to the center. We will no longer be isolated from the surrounding star systems. We will need to get ready to introduce ourselves to our galactic neighbors.

> Some of our biggest advances have come from the retro-engineering of UFO technology.

Beyond Earth: UFOs and Other Star Systems

The rebirth of the world and the ushering in of a new age presents a whole new galactic landscape for us to explore. The time for Earth-centered narcissism is over. We will be forced to admit once and for all that there are other intelligent beings out there in the universe who have been visiting Earth for some time and who are quite possibly living among us right now. The UFO sightings and abductions that have been occurring since time immemorial will finally make sense. The fact is that our galactic neighbors have been visiting Earth for millions of years. We already discussed the Anunnaki, who manipulated the genetics of Earth's primates and created Adam, the first human race. UFO sightings date as far back as the Rama Empire of Northern India and Pakistan, which developed approximately 15,000 years ago on the Indian subcontinent: At this time, according to ancient Indian texts, there existed flying machines called *vimanas*. In other words, the skies of India were

> Our galactic neighbors have been visiting Earth for millions of years.

> High-ranking government officials have been privy to knowledge of alien contact here on Earth for a long time.

once filled with UFOs. Alexander the Great encountered these UFOs as he attempted to cross the Indus River into India in 329 BC. Gleaming silver flying shields swooped down on his cavalry several times, making his own soldiers as well as the enemy flee for their lives. He had another such encounter when he invaded and conquered Tyre, an ancient Phoenician city on the eastern Mediterranean Sea in present-day southern Lebanon. It would appear that the great soldier had some alien help!

And of course there are the countless records of UFO sightings throughout history, up to and including the infamous Roswell Incident. There is still a great deal of speculation that the government has been trying to cover up these incidents. High-ranking government officials have actually been privy to knowledge of alien contact here on Earth for a long time. Supporting documents indicate that President Eisenhower himself even met with aliens before he left office. Henry W. McElroy, Jr, a retiring state representative from New Hampshire, saw an official brief to President Eisenhower stating that there was a continuing presence of extraterrestrial beings in the United States of America. It was suggested that President Eisenhower meet with such alien representatives in February of 1954. Finally, American astronauts Edgar Mitchell, Gordon Cooper, Buzz Aldrin, and Neil Armstrong have all had sightings of extraterrestrial spacecraft but were advised by the U.S. government not to discuss any of their experiences. Although they will never admit to this, agencies such as NASA are in the business of gathering intelligence and data relating to encounters with UFOs and ETs. Is it possible that they know something we don't?

> Archaeological discoveries and monuments point to visitors from space.

German author Erich von Däniken was one of the first to come forward with historical proof of extraterrestrial visits to Earth. His book *Chariots of the Gods* reveals how various archaeological discoveries and monuments point to visitors from space, sojourners who came to Earth as developers to build magnificent structures, cultivate gardens, and simply relish the temperate climate that made the entire planet a virtual Garden of Eden. In *Twilight of the Gods*, von Däniken advises us to prepare for their return, and states that they may already be here. Author Zecharia Sitchin is another proponent of the ancient astronaut hypothesis, and has been educating the public about the alternative history of ancient humanity and the extraterrestrial influence on our planet.

> We all have the opportunity to get back to that primordial Garden if we drop the fear consciousness and proceed with the higher vibrations of love.

I went to one of his lectures in Philadelphia in 2010. The room was packed with a very intelligent audience that hardly seemed representative of the fringe element usually associated with belief in UFOs and aliens. The public is continuously looking for information on the subject of extraterrestrials and the true history of our planet. Decision-makers and people in power are likely afraid of what the reaction would be if the truth came out. What they don't realize is that we all have the opportunity to get back to that primordial Garden if we drop the fear consciousness and proceed with the higher vibrations of love.

Then again, I can think of a few neighborhoods on Earth that might frighten our extraterrestrial cousins. Jeffrey Seelman, an instructor at International Metaphysical University, hosts a radio show and often interviews experts on UFOs. According to Jeffrey, there seems to be a general consensus that the aliens view our planet as a violent place, and are concerned about our planet shifting closer to their star systems. Remember that we have the instincts and brutishness of our animal DNA combined with the psychic powers of our alien ancestors. This is

> Aliens view our planet as a violent place.

quite a lethal combination, especially if one is not of the right consciousness. The aliens are right to be concerned about the consciousness of our planet; we have had a very violent history indeed. If we cannot get along with each other, how could live in peace with them, a race so utterly different from our own? Jeffrey also explained that the inhabitants of other planets are just plain curious about Earth. I know several people who have had encounters with UFOs—none quite so riveting as the one my friend Janet Russell had in 1962. She not only saw one; she was abducted.

It was late March of 1962 when she was driving north on Route 112 in Medford, New York, to see her obstetrician. Janet was 22 years old at that time, and pregnant. The road, which is now a congested artery, connects the north and south shores of Long Island, and was still largely desolate at that point. As Janet was driving she pulled over to the side of the road to glance at what appeared to be a large light in the sky. It resembled the moon, except that it was three times larger, and purple. At this point she lost an hour of time that she could not account for once she arrived at her appointment. Janet appeared to be sunburned; the skin on her face was actually peeling even though it was a chilly, March day in New York. The doctor remarked that she looked like she had just come back from a Florida vacation. About two weeks after the incident she read in a local paper that two policemen also saw the same thing. She knew at that point that she hadn't been imagining things.

After her experience Janet suddenly became very psychic and also developed an intense interest in UFOs and the paranormal. She still had no memory of what had occurred that night, until 33 years later, when she was regressed by the late Dr. Jean Mundy, a prominent psychologist and UFO/alien-abduction researcher in New York who worked with the late Dr. John Mack, a Harvard professor and psychiatrist, and the late Budd Hopkins, author and pioneer UFO/abduction researcher. The regression ultimately helped Janet remember her abduction experience that chilly, March day back in 1962.

She eventually recalled being taken aboard a craft, entering through what resembled a large eye that opened up on the underside. Her abductors did not speak any words. She was told telepathically that she would not be harmed. Janet was brought into a room and was shown petri dishes with human embryos in them. She was then led into a room that was full of a fog-like mist. There she met seven beings, one human and six aliens. The human was tall and Nordic-looking, and seemed to be the leader. Janet noted that he was very handsome, although when she looked at him from the side, he appeared to be a hologram. A small, thin wire was placed into her arm, and she heard what sounded like two separate recordings, one a human voice speaking rapidly, and another just a grunting sound. The tall leader said that this wire would give her knowledge that she would know what to do with when the time was right. Now, on her upper right arm there is actually a thin, cylindrical, 1-inch-long divot. Janet's daughter, with whom she was pregnant at the time of the abduction, has a similar mark on her leg, and she is also very psychic. Ever since her UFO experience, Janet has never doubted for one minute that we are not alone in the universe.

There is some speculation that alien abductions are really just attempts at mind control in order to neutralize our free-will consciousness and bring us through this shift without our posing any risk to the galaxy; others claim that such mind control is meant to make us passive so that aliens can more easily take control of our planet. This is one of the main reasons that our transformation into higher consciousness needs to be of the right vibration. The vibrations from love are the most refined and resilient, so we will need to stay attuned to these vibrations if we want to stay at the top of the frequency food chain. Some of these worlds that will open up to us will be thousands of years ahead of us, so it's important that we be able to ascertain whether we are in the company of beneficent beings or those of a lower vibration. Protecting and defending our own energy will be of utmost importance when we meet our galactic neighbors. Not all alien contact will be positive; there will always be a faction out there that seeks to conquer and control.

The empowering shift and our awakening into transformed energetic beings will finally reveal the truth to us.

Now you can see how the psychic evolution prepares us for the empowering shift of our planet into a different realm of consciousness: Yes, the shift will also charge our planet's chakras. There is one main chakra center on each continent, and many minor ones scattered all over the world. Major Earth chakra centers, such as those at Mt. Shasta, California; Lake Titicaca, South America; Uluru-Katatjuta, Australia; Glastonbury-Shaftesbury, England; the Great Pyramid, Egypt; Mount Sinai and the Mount of Olives, Israel; and Mt. Kailas, Tibet, will spin with new, vibrant energy. Earth's ley lines, her energetic "grid," will glow and radiate with light. The true chronicle of our planet and our race as humans has been cloaked behind religions, myths, and primal fears for centuries, but the empowering shift and our awakening into transformed energetic beings will finally reveal the truth to us. There is no separateness, only a unity of diversity. Everything—our planet, the human race, the cosmos itself—comes from the one Creator God who will finally lift the veil to the eternal life of the spirit. Indeed, "the old order of things has passed away" (Revelation 21:4). The physical world may pass away someday, but the spirit is eternal and will always remain a part of the universe. And, as it turns out, it is a very big universe indeed.

What we are today comes from our thoughts of yesterday, and our present thoughts build our life of tomorrow: Our life is the creation of our mind.

—Buddha

Index

O

O'Donnell, Mary P., 89, 165, 167-168

Ophiuchus, 196-198

Out-of-body experiences, 33, 34, 129-132, 163

P

Parallel lives, 85

Past lives, 85

Phobias, 89

Physical plane body, 76

Physical senses, 47

Physical thought consciousness, 27

Physio-spiritual makeup, 17, 18

Pine cones, 126-127

Pineal gland, 61, 125-132

Piscean age, 30, 196, 201-202

Pituitary gland, 62, 125

Politics, 207-208

Prana, 21, 183

Privacy, 148-154

Protection, 148-154

Psi balls, 158

Psi flu, 18

Psychic ability, 47, 48, 53

Psychic attack, 18

Psychic eye, 39

Psychic knowing, 83

Psychic malfunctions, 161-199

Psychic mediums, 193

Psychic sense of taste, 57

Psychic smell, 55-56

Psychic touch, 59-60, 155-156

Psychic-logical problems, 106

Psychometry, 59-60, 155-156

Q

Quantum healing, 164-168

Quetzalcoatl, 24

Quickening, 47-71, 73, 74, 85, 121

R

Rainbow children, 44-46, 152, 162, 163

Rapid Eye Technology, 108

Rebalancing, 90-96

Rebirth pains, 104-106

Regression, 86-87

Reiki, 84, 89-90, 182

Reincarnation and Biology, 88

Relationships, 147

Remote viewing, 44, 61, 154-155

Removing blocks, 90-96

Responsibility, 143-144

Rife, Dr. Royal R., 169

Rig Veda, 182

About the Author

Lisa Barretta is a practicing astrologer, intuitive counselor, certified Reiki practitioner, and researcher in the fields of consciousness and psychic abilities. Her ability in astrological delineation, coupled with her uncanny intuitive insight, has secured a loyal following throughout the United States, Canada, the United Kingdom, and the Middle East. In the past 30 years she has developed her client base strictly by word of mouth.

Drawing on knowledge from past life incarnations along with a life-long practice of the esoteric arts helped Lisa open the portal to self-discovery and transformation. Through her own personal journey she has tapped into the realms of the higher dimensions, the insights from which she shares for the first time in this book.

Lisa is also the author of *The Street Smart Psychic's Guide to Getting a Good Reading*, an informative and at times humorous book that offers insider advice on how to tap into the world of psychic energy. She also gives you a peek into what it is like to be the psychic reader on the *other* side of the tarot cards, crystal ball, and tea leaves.

Lisa resides with her family in Philadelphia, Pennsylvania.